A JOURNEY TO INDEPENDENCE

Second Edition

Tiffani Harvey

Written Words Publishing LLC
14189 E Dickinson Drive, Unit F
Aurora, CO 80014
www.writtenwordspublishing.com

A Journey to Independence © 2015 by Tiffani Harvey
Second Edition

Published by Written Words Publishing LLC August 31, 2023

ISBN: 978-1-961610-05-7 (paperback)
ISBN: 978-1-961610-06-4 (eBook)

Library of Congress Control Number: 2023914306

Cover Designed by Written Words Publishing LLC

Manufactured and printed in the United States of America

Table of Contents

Foreword

The reason for this book is to help people who want to make their own choices. The author writes about her own mistakes so readers can avoid making the same mistakes. She wants readers to learn how to make their own choices and know what kind of questions they should ask before making a choice. This book is written for:

Middle School and High School students

Victims of violence

People who have disabilities

Family members of people with disabilities

Powers of Attorney and Guardians

Payees

Advocates

Caregivers

She wants to help people learn to ask questions and get answers before making big choices.

She wants to help people get as much independence as their health will allow.

She wants to help everyone to save money and buy only what they can afford!

She suggests that you read and understand everything you are asked to sign. If you don't understand, don't sign or ask someone *you trust* if they understand and agree before you sign.

Acknowledgements

I need to start by thanking Mariaelena Wareham and her staff. It is from watching her organization that I felt the need to write my story.

Next, I want to thank my parents, especially my mom, Judy Singer. She helped me remember a lot of what I wanted to share. We spent many hours on the phone and she spent many hours proofreading my work! Thank you, Mom!

Then there's Eli Harvey. Eli started off as my prayer partner and neighbor who lived across the street. Eli has seen me through the best and worst of times. He's still here! *He's wonderful! I will love him always!*

I want to thank my good friends Randall Luce and Carol M Fender who have been here for me from the beginning.

I want to thank the late Cheryl Corkrum and Terry Orr Neve who prayed for me from the very beginning.

I want to thank all of my proofreaders over the years. They include: The late Allan Orr, Janet Coleman, Linda Noble, Jennifer Huseland, and Holly and Paul Hyndman.

(If you know someone who proofread this book and was not listed, let Tiffani know so she can add them to the list. Thank you.)

I want to thank Pastor John and Sandy Repsold and Pastor Neil and Carol Anderson for their spiritual help the last 6-7 years of this journey.

I'd like to thank Ted Medina for helping me on the computer and going beyond job requirements to help me.

I want to thank Lance Morehouse for helping me emotionally when the "system" would anger me so badly and he would help calm me down.

I would like to thank the seven people who took the time to be interviewed. These people wish to remain nameless.

I want to thank Sue Eller who introduced me to Smashwords.

I want to thank Leona Gow for the many times she has saved me time and money.

Finally, I want to thank the Author of Life—the Lord!

Practical Living: How to Make Everyday Choices (and Stick to Your Choices)

Introduction

As you read this, it is important to understand my view of life. Growing up, people told me I could not do things. Why? I was disabled. As an adult, I got to make my own choices since I had no guardian. I was able to make mistakes and learn from them.

Since 1992, I met people who had mental illnesses who wanted to be as independent I was. Since 1996, I met people who had intellectual disabilities come up and say they want to do things that people without disabilities do such as get married or have a paper route.

While growing up, I worked hard to get others to let me make my own choices! I know a lot of adults who don't make their own choices. I think adults should make their own choices. Adults that don't make their own choices have a guardian or a Power of Attorney make big choices in their life.

In the following pages:

First, I share my life.

Second, I explain how I make my choices.

Third, I write to the individual who wants to apply the information.

Fourth and finally, I write to the person who assists the individual in making choices.

I am a firm believer in health:

- Prevention
- Taking Vitamins
- Eating Healthy
- Exercising
- Taking prescription medicine

- Choosing your own doctors

I believe it's everyone's responsibility to be as healthy as they possibly can!

Being healthy includes avoiding:

- Drugs
- Alcohol
- Tobacco

Being healthy can include cutting back on:

- Salt
- Sugar
- Caffeine

I believe a Powers of Attorney and guardians can be good for medical and health reasons. A guardian can give messages to and from the patient and the doctor.

Be Safe

I support the right of adults with disabilities to make their own choices and make their own mistakes. I believe it is important to keep an open mind. "Keeping an open mind" means you are willing to change your mind if you find out someone has a better idea than you.

If someone is worried that what you are doing is unhealthy or dangerous, think about doing something else.

If you speak slowly or if it is hard to understand what you say, it might be best to have a power of attorney or a guardian. Why? People who can speak clearly and quickly can communicate your needs or wants *faster*! To a doctor and other professionals, "Time is money!"

I chose to write this book after many people who have intellectual disabilities asked me how I got to do things that their guardian wouldn't let them do. This includes:

- Getting married
- Going to college
- Handling my own money

I thought I could reach more people by writing this book instead of telling my story to one person at a time. I also thought people could go back and look something up if they didn't remember what I said.

I write from the point of view of a person with intellectual disabilities. If I don't know about something, I ask others who do know about that topic. Some information is constantly changing, but the source is the same. So, you can look up the latest information.

Practical Living: How to Choose

Childhood

I was born with partial seizures. I always felt them coming on. The left side of my body does not work very well. I have a rose colored birthmark on the right side of my face. I have vision issues. I also have a conceptual learning disability.

I had very few friends because my parents were embarrassed by other kids in special education. My parents wanted me to have friends who had no disabilities, but the able bodied kids teased me. I tried to be friends with all the adults my parents invited over including the professionals. I never understood why they never approved. I thought my parents would allow them to be my friend because they had no disabilities and my parents let them in the house. My parents were upset with me, but I never understood why.

I was on a lot of medicines growing up. I had lots of side effects. Side effects are unwanted things that happen as result of taking medicine. Side effects I had:

- Feeling half asleep
- Hard time focusing
- Hard time understanding schoolwork

A doctor told my mom I would not walk or talk. God proved the doctor wrong. I walk with a limp, but I don't use a walker or a cane, and I talk very well.

Family Life

One important thing my parents taught me was being faithful to each other and to me when life got hard.

My mom has Multiple Sclerosis (MS). She had a mild case of it. Over the years, her MS had gone in and out of remission.

"Remission" means the symptoms of a disability disappear. When the disability comes "out of remission" the symptoms reappear. When I was two years old, my mom had to use a walker because her MS was out of remission. There were times she would have double vision for a week or two, and then her vision was fine again.

When I was in grade school, my mom was a stay-at-home mom. When I entered middle school, she got a job. She worked for about 13 years but had to stop when she was no longer in remission.

Dad worked at Kaiser Aluminum. He rotated shifts. He worked day shift, swing shift, and the graveyard shift. He also worked a lot of extra hours. My dad has no disabilities. Growing up, Dad and I frustrated each other a lot because we didn't understand each other. This was hard on Mom. For example, I always sang in the school choir. I would tell Dad 1-3 months *before* a concert thinking he could plan ahead to come to my concert. I thought God and family were more important than a job.

My value system was and still is that God and family are more important than a job.

As an adult, I started to understand—you can live in the same house, go to the same church, but still have totally different values.

I am an only child. My parents were afraid of having another child with disabilities. They have even said to me, "Do you want another disabled child like you in the world?!"

This is one of my beliefs: Stand up for what you believe in!

I learned to stand up for myself and voice my opinions. I always knew I was special in God's eyes. Everybody is!

My Grandparents

We went and visited my grandma in Idaho a lot while I was growing up. She was always there for everyone. She was my dad's mom. As her eight kids grew up and moved all across the country, she stayed in contact with everyone. (These were the days before cell phones and the internet.) Grandma was great at having family reunions. She died in a hospital from heart failure when I was in the 7th grade. This was my first experience with death.

I was close to my grandparents on my mom's side. My grandpa worked on a farm. Grandma was a homemaker. We would go visit my grandparents more often than my other grandma. The main thing my grandparents taught me: family comes first. Whenever us grandkids came, we were the center of their attention. That helped me have strong family values. Later in life, Grandpa suffered from Alzheimer's disease and Grandma got skin cancer. She died at my aunt's house in 1990, a few weeks after I graduated from high school. My aunt and two cousins took care of them along with an agency called Hospice until Grandma died.

My family took care of my grandpa until it got *very hard*. My mom and aunt put Grandpa in an adult family home.

It is my belief that the women of the family should take care of their older relatives *if* the family can afford it. We could afford it and I wanted to.

There were a few problems with me taking care of him:

1. No one ever asked my grandpa.
2. I was being told, "You're disabled. You can't take care of him!"
3. My aunt and mom were assuming that my grandpa would be embarrassed if I took care of him.
4. His generation always made sure that the family took care of sick family members even if that meant that older

relatives had to move into another family member's home.

It would have been respectful _to ask_ my grandpa before placing him in the adult family home and later moving him into a nursing home.

My grandpa died in early 1993. After all three of my grandparents died, there were no more family reunions. For a few years after they died, we stayed in touch by calling each other and by writing letters. Eventually, the letter writing stopped and later everyone stopped calling each other.

I never let my disabilities get in my way or stop me from doing what I wanted to do. I wanted to be like everyone else. I wanted to ride a bike, swim, sing in the choir, and play sports. As an adult, I wanted to do all the things other able bodied adults did such as being a wife, a stay-at-home parent, move away from my parents, go to college, get a part-time job, and have a driver's license. _I wanted to find out for myself what I could or could not do_!

As a kid, I never learned to ride a bike without training wheels, so I don't ride. I think swimming is fun, but swimming alone is dangerous. I remember I was seven years old in a friend's backyard pool and I had a seizure. A five-year-old neighbor was keeping my head above water while yelling for her mom to help. The neighbor's mom called my mom. After that, I only wanted to go to pools that were easy to get out of. Why? Safety: because I knew lifeguards were around.

Once you find out something is unhealthy or dangerous, find a healthier or safer way to do it or don't do it.

"Accommodation" means finding a way that works around your disability or disabilities that allows a person to do things independently. An example would be people who are blind using a white cane or a service animal to walk around.

Church Background

The only reason some of the kids went to church was, they were forced to.

When I entered 10th grade, I met my first boyfriend. He invited me to his church. My parents said I could go. That was October 1987, and I was 16.

**The last seven churches I have gone to have been my choice; I *chose* to leave my parents' religion. They have the right to choose their religion and where they want to go to church, and so do I! Their religion is different, but it's not necessarily wrong! I want you to feel good about your choices! My parents allowed me to change to my boyfriend's church and I went there as long as I wanted to—for ten years!

School

When I was in 3rd grade, a kid said, "Fxxx you," so I asked mom what does "Fxxx you" mean? She slapped me. That was the first time my mom ever hit me. I learned quickly, don't ask my parents questions, hide in the church, and stick with people who have disabilities. Why? Kids without disabilities use bad words. Using bad words got my face slapped. Since I never wanted to be slapped again, I stayed away from kids without disabilities. I was so sheltered that I didn't realize both people with and without disabilities use bad words.

My mom gave the school my medical information and that bothered me! I wanted to keep it private. I felt that only the doctors should have that information. I was afraid the teachers would treat me differently if they knew the specifics of my disabilities. I was right! They treated me differently. My parents and the high school never let me take driver's education! No one ever gave me credit for thinking safely! If I didn't feel safe, I would not drive.

When I entered 6th grade, my parents moved seven miles off the bus line. Even when I was too young to drive, I thought we should have been living on the city bus line so I could have a social life. I worried that I would never drive and that I would never have a social life.

Throughout middle school, I was mad at God, my parents, and the world. Why? I was so frustrated with my disabilities. I felt I was being left out at school and at church because I was not allowed to get a driver's license. Also, no one listened to how I planned to stay safe to prevent an accident.

In 8th grade, a group of female students kept calling me a virgin and I had no idea what "virgin" meant. I kept saying, "No, I'm not!" They finally asked me, "Who did you sleep with?" I told them, "Nobody! That's sick!"

They responded, "Then you're a virgin." I said, "Okay," and I accepted it, and wore the name proudly!

Choir, English, and math were my best subjects when I was in K-6. My grades in English and choir continued to be great in 7-12. My grades in history were always low. History was hard on me emotionally because of all the wars and death. I hate war, guns, and death.

Science and biology were also hard subjects for me. I did not understand formulas for science. Cutting up frogs and other animals in biology made me feel sick, so I tried to forget everything in that class. In the classes I had a really hard time in, I was given a "D" so I could pass and get to the next grade level. Physical Education was also hard. Why? Catching and throwing baseballs, footballs, etc. was hard for me. I had a hard time running because I sprained my ankle falling on the ice so many times. The only sport I liked in school was volleyball. Even though I got hit in the face with the volleyball, I was having fun.

1st – 8th grade: my friends were girls. In 9th – 12th grade my friends were boys. 10th grade was when I became interested in dating men who went to church.

Remember, if it's hard to do some of the things that I write about, there are agencies out there that can help!

If there are other things you need help with, look to see who can teach you. Who you ask depends on what kind of help you need.

What kind of help do you need?

- Advice
- Financial help (help with money) (energy assistance)
- Shopping
- Paperwork
- Something else

Who you ask depends on what it is you need. People or agencies that might be able to help are:

- Family
- Government Agencies
- Nonprofit organizations
- Your place of worship
- Organizations that help people of your faith
- Friends

For example, if I need to get something like milk, or go back to the doctor in the same day, there are a few people I can ask for a ride. If I need help with my homework, I have a different group of people I can ask.

Taking Medicines and Choosing Doctors

Before anyone thinks about living on their own, they might need to prove that they know how to take their medicines, when to take their medicines, and prove that they can be trusted to always take it correctly!

At age 12, my parents trusted me to take my own seizure medicine. In the summer of 1986, I went to visit my cousins. This went on for seven days. I *accidently* forgot to take my medicines. When I realized I had forgotten to take them, I told my aunt. She asked, "Are you having any seizures?" I said, "No." When Mom and I were driving home, I told her I stopped taking my medicines and she nearly drove off the road. Mom was scared saying, "And you are not having withdrawal symptoms or seizures?" I answered, "No! What are withdrawal symptoms?!" I *never* should have asked because I trusted God to heal me.

However, being the curious person I am, I asked, "What are withdrawal symptoms?" I got every symptom she told me about.

My parents let me continue taking my medicines because I admitted my mistake. No one thought I would stop taking my medicines again. After all, I'm the one who suffered!

If you are a slow learner, or if you learn by making the same mistakes over and over again, others may want you to have a backup plan.

I graduated in 1990 and I changed my medical doctor. Six to nine months after I graduated, I wanted to be on less seizure medicine. My new medical doctor didn't know me that well and did not know much about seizures, so he disagreed with me.

Finally, six to nine months later, he decided to send me to a doctor who knew more about seizures.

(If your doctor listens to you and will work with you, follow your doctor's advice!)

In 1992, I had an emotional breakdown. I willingly went into the hospital for 14 days and was on a new medicine for three

11

months. Three months later, I asked the doctor if I could stop taking the medicine or if I needed it. The doctor said I could stop!

In 2000, a lot of things were happening:

- A company that made one of my medicines stopped manufacturing it.
- I got a new seizure doctor who never respected me.
- I had a personal crisis in my life.
- I was getting two to three hours of sleep for three weeks.
- The doctor pushed me over the edge.
- I did something harmful that I _never_ should have done without talking to my seizure doctor.
- I had to get my stomach pumped to stay alive.

Knowing how much sleep I had lost, I told my counselor four days before doing something that put me in the emergency room!

I was in the hospital again, this time half willingly. Why? I didn't trust my counselor since she didn't believe me when I told her I needed help. She waited too long to get me the help I needed. I was also in a different hospital and they were mean to me. They took me off of all my seizure medicines and, when I did have a seizure, they told me I was faking it. Those doctors in the hospital should have known what a seizure was even if they didn't know anything about seizure medicines. They should have been smart enough to talk to my seizure doctor and never should have taken me off my seizure medicine!

In the hospital, I was diagnosed with two more disabilities—bipolar and panic/anxiety disorder. I had known about the panic/anxiety attacks for a long time. I chose not to go to the doctor, and I handled it in a very foolish way. I didn't want to get help. A client at the mental health agency was the cause of my anxiety/panic attacks, and the agency was legally unable to protect me. What I needed was the agency to make sure our appointments were at different times so we wouldn't be in the building at the same time. I knew this person went there, and I felt the agency was treating me as if I didn't know anything or that they didn't care about my safety! I did get help once my medical insurance allowed me to go to a different agency!

When I got out of the hospital, I was able to take my medicine myself. Why? I think they let me because I had gone to my counselor and asked for help many times which made the problem the company's fault. *If* I had said, "I'm fine. I don't need help," when I really did need help, I probably would have had to live in an adult family home until I could be trusted again because everyone would have been worried about me, and I might have been forced to have a guardian. That is why it is important to know your needs, wants, and limitations.

Regarding reducing medicine: If you want the doctor to reduce your medicines, have a reason! It is the same with changing doctors or avoiding certain doctors—have a reason! Since I have problems with my eyes, it was very stupid of me to go to the eye doctor every three to five years. The doctor wants me to come in every three months. I hate anything in my eyes; however, it is very important for *my* vision.

The third thing you have to do: *Go to all of your doctor's appointments and reschedule if you can't make those appointments*!

When I graduated from high school, I was in the process of choosing which doctors to keep and which doctors to change. For a while, I saw the same kind of doctor twice for the same thing. He gave my mom and me the information since we were both making different appointments. I got to the appointments I made by taking the city bus or disability van.

A year later, I changed my doctor because:

- I knew of a doctor in my church
- To start my life separate from my parents

I kept my parents in my life but wanted some distance which is why I got different doctors. When I changed my doctors, I kept it a secret for six months. I wanted my doctors *to know me*!

There are doctor's offices I hate to go to. Recently, I grew up enough to at least go to the eye doctor every two to three years. I am the one who will suffer if I refuse to go. I should go more often, but I am the one who will reap the consequences—good and bad!

TO CHOICE MAKER: If you want to be more independent with your medicines, talk with your pharmacist and the doctor who prescribes it to you.

Questions should include:

- What is this medicine for?
- What is it supposed to do for me?
- What are the possible side effects of this medicine?
- You must tell the prescribing doctor about *all* the side effects you have from a medication.
- Tell *all* your doctors all the medication you are taking.

If you have any side effects that you refuse to live with, tell your support team and healthcare professionals what those side effects are so they can find medicines that don't have those side effects! For example, there is a new device that can help reduce or stop seizures; however, it would affect my voice. I would rather live with the seizures than mess up my voice. Why? I love to sing. I also hate medicines that will make me tired unless the medicine is to help me sleep.

Know your boundaries. If you are not taking a medicine for the purpose of making you tired, there might be another medicine that does the same job, but will not cause sleepiness.

All medicines have side effects!

Regarding taking your own medicines:

- Ask if you can take the medicines out of the bottle with supervision.
- If you have been taking it out of the bottle *correctly* with supervision, ask if you can take your medicine without

14

supervision. If they say, "No," find out why!

If you want to consider changing doctors, here is one way to do it. There are many ways. This is my way:

1) Research/look up four doctors.
   A) It gives you practice at shopping around for the best of everything (products and services) even when you have the best.
   B) If you do have the best, you will be able to trust your support team even more!
2) Ask friends about how their doctors treat them. If friends have good experiences, they usually will tell their friends. If they had a bad experience, they will probably protect you by warning you not to go to that place and tell you why!
3) When you call a new doctor's office, ask if they will accept your "medical insurance." Make sure you know who your insurance company or companies are and that every doctor you have accepts your insurance. If you don't have any medical insurance, ask if they will charge you on a "sliding scale fee." Sliding scale fee is when they charge you based on how much money you earn. If they accept sliding scale fee, then ask them how much they will charge you!
4) What services does each doctor provide? Do they provide the services that you need?
5) If it is important to you that you and your doctor believe the same way on certain things, then ask them! (For an example: Some people may want a doctor who does not believe in abortion.)
6) Has the doctor ever been sued for malpractice?
7) If he/she has been sued, how many times and for what reason?
8) Finally, ask any questions that are important to you! If you need help thinking of questions, ask your support

team to help you think of questions you would want to ask. Your list of questions should reflect your needs. (These questions can include your belief system if that's important to you!)

Personally, I know what kind of doctors I want to have. They are usually in a certain age range. I choose doctors who are a little older. They seem to have more experience and nothing seems to shock or surprise them. I also look at their personality.

TO SUPPORT TEAM: If the choice maker comes to you and says, "I want to take my own medicine," talk it over with them to see if they really understand what they are asking for. If they understand, allow them to take it with supervision! If they have been supervised and they ask to take it without supervision, ask them different questions.

If they want to change doctor(s), give them information about their doctor and four other doctors who do that kind of work if your person with a disability asks you! Get four doctors for each kind of doctor! Find out why they need/want to change doctors.

TO BOTH OF YOU: Talk to each other! Find out why your support team doesn't let you take your medicines *at this time*, and find out why it's important to your protected person for them to take their own medicines. You two might disagree with each other, but if you do, find a compromise—something that gives both of you a little bit of what you want.

If you, the choice maker, doesn't want to take prescription medicine:

- Get information about alternative medicines.
- Talk to your doctors if you are interested in trying alternative medicines _before_ taking prescription medication!
- Eat healthy.
- Take vitamins. (Let your pharmacist and all your doctors know what vitamins you want to take and why!)

16

- Tell them what vitamins you are taking.

If you take vitamins, have your doctor prescribe them to you, so if you ever have to go to the hospital or move into an assistive living facility you will still get to take your vitamins!

- Exercise

Do all of the above things consistently!

If the choice maker wants to reduce or change medicine(s), tell the doctor the reason for wanting to change it, especially if the medication is working. My medication was working but made me so tired that I couldn't do anything. Once I moved onto the bus line/disability van service is *when* I noticed how tired I was. As long as I lived in the country with no social life, I never noticed how tired I was because I was so bored. If your doctor isn't listening to you, your support team should make the doctor listen and understand you! The doctor might not be able to give you what you ask for, but if he/she is smart, they will tell you why!

I became so independent that when I ended up in the hospital in 2000, I didn't have an advocate to tell the hospital staff that I couldn't open childproof medicine bottles, so when I got out of the hospital, I had to find someone who could open my medicine bottles for me.

The hospital assumed that since most people enjoy watching TV, I would also. I *hate* TV! Why? Too much sex, violence, and bad words! The staff showed no respect for my religious beliefs and no understanding of my physical limitations. When I got out of the hospital, I found someone to speak for me in case this happens again!

Part of being independent is knowing **when to ask questions and when to accept help!**

It's smart for everyone to choose two people that they trust to make healthcare choices for them in case they ever become unable to make their own choices.

In order for professionals to know who is allowed to make choices for you, you must make it a legal document. The document becomes legal when the document is taken to a notary so they can watch you sign the document. The decision maker is only allowed to make decisions when the creator of the legal paper is unable to make their choices!

If I can't make my own healthcare choices, *I want to choose the person who will make my choices **when I can't!***

I have made this document and I have had to use this document a couple of times!

I feel safe knowing **who** will speak for me *when* I'm unable!

Making Choices By Setting Boundaries

We make choices every day. The choices you make create *who you are as a person*. We choose our friends, where we want to live, work, etc. We also make lifestyle choices by the boundaries we set. "Boundaries" means what you will and will not do. "Boundaries" also means what you will and won't accept from someone else.

People know who we are by what we will and won't do. We are also known by who our friends are.

When thinking about what you want your boundaries to be, think about how you were raised. Do you want to do what your family did? I might try to do all the good things my parents did, and I would try to not make the same mistakes they made. As time goes by, I would see if I needed to change any of my choices and why. I'd make different choices and set new boundaries if and when they needed to be changed.

How does a person choose their boundaries? Find out what you value most. Ideas are your health, your faith, safety, morality, etc. *You* must set *your* boundaries! Don't give into "peer pressure." Peer pressure means doing something because someone wants you to even though you don't want to.

Here is an example of how I made a choice about swearing:

1) Would I care if my church friends heard me swear?
2) Do my parents swear?
3) Is swearing a healthy thing to do?
4) Is it legal?
5) Are there any rewards to swearing?
6) Could anything bad happen if I swore?

The answers to the questions above helped me decide not to swear. The only time I have used swear words is when I was so angry that I couldn't find any other way to express my anger to anyone! But I don't want to make it a habit! Last, but not least, the Bible tells us to use positive words to encourage each other.

19

This is how I make choices on any subject:

- First, how would I feel if one of my Christian friends knew I was doing this?
- Second, is it healthy?
- Third, is it legal?
- Fourth, can I pay for it?

I am always willing to listen to how other people set their boundaries, what their boundaries are, and the reason for those boundaries. I won't let someone force me into their way of thinking. For example, it took me ten years to understand health issues. Now that I understand health issues and why it's important, I am a very strong supporter of being healthy. I respect other people's right to make their own choices even if their choices are unhealthy. However, I have the right to choose friends who make healthy choices.

The only time I will force someone to make healthy choices is if my employer tells me I must! Usually, I give very strong suggestions with very good reasons to make good choices about health. The more a person means to me, the more it matters to me that they make healthy choices and stay healthy!

Our boundaries help us choose our friends, our hobbies, and what we do with our time!

When talking to your support team and healthcare professionals, ask them what their boundaries are and how they decided on their boundaries. Respect everyone's right to set their own boundaries.

When you have set your boundaries, tell your support team what your reasons are!

Remember, your boundaries make up who you are as a person! They tell people what you will and will not accept!

Lifestyle Choices

We all make choices in life. Some choices identify who we are. Our choices tell others if we are:

- Godly or ungodly
- Moral or immoral
- Ethical or unethical
- Professional or unprofessional

We might treat different people in different ways.

How do you want to be known? The next few chapters will look at some big areas of life.

Choose your lifestyle. Be open to reasonable change. (For example, as cigarettes get more expensive, is it smart to continue smoking? Another example would be changing jobs. If there's a problem at work, do you change departments, look for a different job, or do something else?)

Religion

As a child, I had to go to church with my parents. I had no choice, but the church taught me to be a moral person. When I got into middle school, my friends at church were doing all the things the kids at school did. The church teenagers were also teasing me about my disabilities. They teased me about the way I walked and the way I looked. As a child, I did not expect to get teased at church.

When I was in the 10th grade, someone at school invited me to his church and I gladly went! The youth group was big and they did not tease me because of my disabilities. I told my mom I wanted to attend that church. My parents talked it over and said that would be okay.

Six months after attending this church, I chose to accept Jesus Christ into my heart, instead of only having the knowledge of Jesus Christ in my head. Jesus is one main reason I can smile even though I have multiple disabilities.

How to choose a faith:

- First, realize that this is a personal choice.
- Second, watch people who believe in different religions/faiths. How does faith affect their life? Are they usually happy, sad, angry, stuck up, joyful, and do they look like they have peace?
- Third, choose 10-20 people in each faith and watch them. Why 10-20? No one should base their choice on one example.
- Fourth, don't easily change your mind if you are happy with your life!
- Fifth, know yourself well enough to know if a faith will or won't work for you.

Here is an example of one faith that would never work for me. I am a very politically active person who will stand up for religious values and the rights of people who have disabilities. There is a religion that avoids politics. That would drive me crazy! I vote and call politicians on the City, County, State, and the Federal levels. Knowing how politically active I am, I could never be part of that faith! Also, I am perfectly happy with the faith I have, so why look? This is worth saying again! If you are happy with your faith, don't look for a new one!

However, it's always smart to watch how your family and friends react when bad things happen (and remember their reactions). How does their faith help them when bad things happen to them?

There are people who share their faith with everyone. You can choose to share your faith, you can keep quiet about your faith until someone asks you, or you can choose to avoid conversations of faith! It's your choice!

Smoking and Electronic Smoking

Everyone I knew were nonsmokers until I started middle school. If anyone smoked while I was in elementary school, I didn't know it. Therefore, I chose to never smoke.

After I made the choice to never smoke, I found out my dad was a smoker for ten years, and he stopped smoking overnight for me, so I would never start.

Other reasons I chose to be a nonsmoker was, I love to sing and smoking would hurt my voice, and it stinks. I also read in the Bible that the body is the temple of God. Since my body is the temple of God, I don't want to hurt my body.

TO CHOICE MAKER: Here are some things to think about when making this choice:

A) The first is money.
B) The second is, it can make a smoker get a horrible cough known as "smoker's cough."
C) Third, smoking too much will turn a smoker's teeth and fingernails yellow. When that happens, smokers look older than they really are!
D) The fourth thing to consider is, do you want to play music or afterschool sports? Smoking makes it very hard to breathe! If you smoke it will be really hard to succeed in music or sports.
E) The fifth thing to look at is health. Smoking makes your lungs black! The longer you smoke, the blacker they get and the harder it will be to breathe. Smoking can cause many lung problems including lung cancer. I personally know someone who had to have their voice box taken out because of cancer caused by smoking.
F) The sixth thing about smoking is, it's socially unacceptable.

At the time this book was written, smoking was becoming more and more socially unaccepted in the

USA! It is still legal. All 50 States are trying to make smoking illegal.

   Author's suggestions: If you have an opinion about any law the City, County, State, or Feds are writing, call or e-mail your politicians.

G) When I was in 12th grade, the athletes and music students had to sign a contract. The athletes could not smoke. The music students' contract had nothing in it about smoking. However, both athletes and musicians got letters on their high school jackets. The coaches complained about there being two different sets of rules. So, in the middle of the semester, the choir teacher came into class and said, "If you smoke, you will fail this class!" It was too late to change classes. As a nonsmoker, I gathered all the smokers together and we went to the vice principal's office. My main issue was that the teacher was breaking the contract. If we had to obey the contract, so did the teacher and school! If they wanted to change the contract next semester that was fine, but the school had to obey this contract! We won, and the new contract said music students could not smoke. Why did I help the students? They helped me by signing a petition to get a Bible Club or class. I wanted the Bible Club to be able to advertise just like other clubs did.

H) The eighth thing about smoking is addiction. I have a couple of recovering alcoholic friends who are also "recovering smokers." A "recovering smoker" is someone who was addicted to smoking and has stopped smoking but will always be tempted to smoke. Two of my friends told me that to stop smoking is harder than trying to stop drinking. One has stopped smoking and the other one still smokes.

Both my friends explained the process of quitting is like going through mental and physical withdrawal symptoms. The best way mental withdrawal symptoms have been explained to me is that a smoker always needs to have something in their mouth and in their hand.

The longer a person smokes, the harder it will be for them to quit when they want to quit. How can you tell if you are addicted to something? For example, with smoking and text messaging, if you feel that you are unable to put the cigarettes or phone down when it's necessary, you're addicted.

There are only two *possible* good things I know about smoking:

A) It is a drug that doesn't alter your mind. Alcohol and illegal drugs alter the mind.
B) The second thing is, I've been told by smokers that "smoking releases stress." (Those same smokers are quick to say, "There are healthier ways to deal with stress without smoking!")

If you are thinking about smoking, ask people you trust, "Why did you start smoking?" Ask a number of people before you make your choice. Chances are if they still smoke, they really want to quit. (Most smokers I have talked to said they started because of peer pressure. Most of the smokers I talked to wish they never started and have quit or want to quit!) Don't start smoking because your friends did!

"Giving into peer pressure" or "being pressured" by those around you to do something that you might not want to do" means doing what others want you to do only so you fit in with the crowd. It's something you would not do if you were by yourself or with a different group of people. Peers can be classmates, coworkers, residents in an adult family home/group home, friends, etc.

We can all take steps to live healthier lives by choosing to be nonsmokers, choosing to use electronic cigarettes, cut back, or quit. If you don't smoke, don't start!

Being a nonsmoker doesn't promise a long life. It increases your chances of enjoying a healthy life!

Through reading this chapter you have learned what questions to ask smokers, ex-smokers, and nonsmokers regarding why they chose to smoke, quit or never start.

So, my question to anyone who is thinking about smoking is, *why* would you want to start?

I have only heard of two people who really enjoy smoking or want to smoke. One of these two made weak attempts to stop smoking because of his nagging wife and his child who has a breathing problem.

I believe smokers must want to quit for themselves! If a smoker stops smoking for someone else, they will probably start smoking again. If someone asks a smoker to stop smoking or never start, please listen to their reason(s) and then make your own choice. It's important and polite for a smoker to tell others why they don't want to quit. If you want to start smoking, it's smart to tell someone why you are choosing to start.

I 100% accept your choice to smoke, cut back, or not smoke at all. The only thing I ask of smokers is to *please show the same respect for nonsmokers that they are willing to show to you*!

RESPECTFUL SMOKING TIPS:

- Don't throw butts on the ground! Throw your cigarettes in ashtrays!
- Be polite!
- If you know there is a nonsmoker around, tell them you want to 'light up.' You can ask a nonsmoker to go somewhere else while you smoke because nonsmokers and ex-smokers can go anywhere. Smokers cannot!
- If there are people around you who have a breathing problem, don't smoke! Their life depends on being in a smoke-free environment. Wait or go somewhere else! You can wait! If your addiction is so bad that you feel the need to have a cigarette when someone around you is on oxygen, it's time to cut back or quit!

- When "hanging out" with a nonsmoking friend, *ask* them would it bother them if you smoke. If it would bother them, then don't smoke. If you can't wait any longer, then let them know, go somewhere else, smoke, and when you are done smoking, go back to your friend.
- When you are outside, make sure the smoke is blowing away from people, and not into other people's faces.
- *Air yourself out before going back inside!

ELECTRONIC SMOKING/E-cigarettes (E-cigs)

For smokers who can't or don't want to quit smoking, there's a new kind of cigarette available. It's an "electronic cigarette." There are also electronic pipes and cigars. These products are also called "smokeless cigarettes."

A lot of businesses that sell electronic cigarettes only want to sell to people who already smoke.

If you have to smoke, there are many benefits and a few risks to using the electronic cigarette, but there are many more dangers to smoking regular tobacco products.

Electronic cigarettes, pipes, and cigars:

- Has nicotine. Nicotine is what makes smoking addictive!
- Has NO tobacco. Tobacco is the ingredient that causes fires! Using electronic devices will never cause house fires or forest fires.
- Doesn't cause secondhand smoke, so only you smoke! You don't have to worry about the people around you!
- It's cheaper *over time*!
- It might reduce the "smoker's cough."

I accept everybody's choices regarding smoking no matter what my choices and opinions are. Why? I want other people to accept and to respect my choices and opinions even if they disagree with me!

How to make your choice about smoking, start smoking, never start smoking, or cut back on smoking? Go through all the questions listed above and below and see if any of these are important to you. In what ways are they important to you? Are they important in starting, cutting back, stopping, or never starting in the first place?

Do your own research! You can ask smokers, ex-smokers, and nonsmokers why they made the choice they made. You can also find information on:

- TV
- Internet
- Newspaper/Magazines
- Place of worship
- Family
- Healthcare professionals

I was tempted to smoke once. I was 34. I had three reasons to continue to be a nonsmoker. I choose not to tell you what they are. However, when I was tempted, I talked to a smoker who told me, 'I was smart for never smoking' and that made me feel good! He helped me stay a nonsmoker.

If you have chosen to stop smoking, you need to plan how you will <u>avoid</u> any temptations to start again. You will need to know what tempts you to smoke. Learn to know when there's a problem and leave before you get a cigarette.

I deal with my stress, anxiety/panic attacks and anger by praying, reading my Bible, fighting for the rights of people who have disabilities, singing, deep breathing, and going for a walk, etc. What I do depends on the situation. The way I lower stress, anxiety, and anger might not help you to lower yours. Find ways that will take your mind off smoking that work for you!

Do you want to say, "No," when someone asks you to go outside and smoke with them? If you want your answer to be "No," find friends who don't smoke. This way you avoid the situation. If you make friends with people who used to smoke, these friends can share with you how they learned to say, "No." They can also encourage you to say, "No."

To the smoker: **Be safe**! Here are some safety tips:

- Never smoke in bed.
- Use a lighter
- Avoid matches.
- Never let children play with cigarette lighters.
- Always keep lighters out of reach of children.
- Always keep cigarettes out of the reach of children.
- If you use matches, put them in an ashtray!
- Finish a cigarette or put it out!
- ***Never leave cigarettes burning when you are done!***
- Make sure cigarettes are out.
- Never throw cigarettes out car windows.
- Never share other people's lit cigarettes.
- Never take cigarette butts out of public ashtrays.

The reason for these last two is health reasons. Stay healthy!

To secondhand smokers: How do smokers treat you? For example, one of my close smoking friends has chosen to be my telephone friend! Another friend who smokes has never respected me or his wife as nonsmokers. When I stopped going to their house, I found I could breathe better and smell things.

If you are looking for a romantic relationship, would it bother you to kiss an ashtray? A smoker's mouth is like an ashtray. If it would bother you, don't get into a romantic relationship with a person who smokes.

TO CHOICE MAKER: Ask questions so you make an educated choice. Here are some questions you can ask:

- How much does it cost?
- What are the health risks?
- Are there any benefits to smoking?
- Why do smokers start?
- Why do ex-smokers quit?

- Why do some people never start smoking?

After asking your own questions, talk to your support team about the answers to the questions you asked. By asking multiple people you will get multiple "real life" opinions regarding the choice to smoke. Below is the research I did!

I asked smokers and ex-smokers, "Why did you start smoking?" The following is a list of answers I got:

- "It relieves my stress."
- "I do not know."
- "My family smoked when I was a child, so I started smoking."
- "I wanted to fit in with the crowd."
- "Peer pressure."
- "There is no good reason, it's stupid!"

TO SUPPORT TEAM: With all the information there is telling people that smoking is bad and to say, "No," to smoking, they don't need to be told by you also. Let them make their own choice. If they choose to smoke, you can let them know that you disagree with their choice, but that you respect their right to make that choice. This gives them a chance to make a good, bad, or neutral choice (depending on how you see it.)

Alcohol

What is alcohol? Alcohol is a **legal** drug. Alcohol is a major ingredient found in beer, wine, liquor, some prescription medicines, and some over-the-counter medicines. Alcohol Pamphlet: Performance Resource Press, Inc., Troy, Michigan 1-800-453-7733. (Referred to as "Alcohol Pamphlet" from now on.)

What does alcohol do to a person? Lowers self-esteem and "lowers self-control which often leads to loud or aggressive behavior." (Alcohol Pamphlet)

Alcohol can change what reality looks like. 'Alcohol can temporarily make a person's sight, hearing, feeling, smelling, and taste buds bad.' Alcohol *can* affect a person's memory, muscle coordination, and judgment, "The bigger the dose, the greater the damage." 'In large doses…effect on the brain can also cause coma, unconsciousness, respiratory failure, and death.' (Alcohol Pamphlet)

A question I have is, 'If alcohol is so dangerous, why have our elected officials allowed alcohol to continue to be legal?' I did get an answer, but the answer is too hard to explain.

I interviewed seven people about alcohol. The questions are about their personal experiences and their opinions about alcohol.

I interviewed a man who is a "recovering alcoholic." "Recovering alcoholic" means a person who is addicted to alcohol who currently stopped drinking. If this person takes another drink, it will be difficult for him stop drinking again. This man started drinking alcohol by choice after he had surgery. As a man in his early 40's, he thought he would know when to stop drinking. He started drinking because he was in pain when he got out of surgery. He wanted off his prescription pain medicine because his girlfriend said she would marry him if he stopped taking it. Against the doctor's advice, he stopped taking the pain medicine and started drinking alcohol to stop his pain.

I, Tiffani, the interviewer am thinking, 'There must be a mix of good and bad things to drinking alcohol because so many people are trying to stop drinking alcohol and more people start drinking. It's been this way throughout history.'

First interview: "As an outsider looking in, what do people think is so fun about drinking?"

He said, "Nice feelings such as loosening up, like taking pain medicine and it is nice on social occasions."

"What are the downsides of drinking alcohol?"

"Getting a hangover, feeling sick the following day. You lose your health because your body does not get the nutrients it needs. You can also lose your family and your job."

"How long has it been since you drank?"

"Eleven years with no relapses at the time of this interview." ("Relapse" means a recovering alcoholic who stopped drinking for a long period of time and starts drinking again.)

"What took you so long before you chose to quit drinking?"

"I got sick three times. The third time, I decided to quit because my stomach was hurting really bad. When I chose to stop drinking, I was given a prescription medicine to take away the good feelings of drinking, and I went into an outpatient treatment program Monday – Friday from 8:00 am – 5:00 pm. The doctor made sure I was ready to stop drinking before he prescribed me that medicine to help me quit. The continuing support or support systems are helping me to stay sober. Counseling and going to Alcoholics Anonymous (AA)."

Another question I asked was, "Is there any such thing as 'responsible drinking'?"

"Absolutely! You *cannot* be an alcoholic *and* a responsible drinker at the same time!"

"Are there any other comments?"

"If you take prescription medicines, ***don't*** drink!" End of interview.

Alcohol affects people differently. Physical, mental, and environmental factors are some of the ways that will determine how people react. Other factors include: Do they have food in their stomach at the time they are drinking, how much they weigh, their tolerance level, their personality and their mood. (Alcohol Pamphlet)

What is social drinking? The term "social drinker/social drinking" can be very confusing. To find out what a social drinker really is, let us look at the doctor's opinion. Social drinkers *don't* drink every day! When they do drink, they space their drinks out for a minimum of one hour.

Some medical professionals say that drinking one glass of red wine is good for people's health. All medical professionals agree that liquor, beer, and white wine are bad. If you want to drink for medical reasons, talk to your pharmacist. He/she is the expert on how prescription medications and over-the-counter medicines interact with alcohol. Ask a pharmacist before you drink red wine!

It is time to interview the second person. It is important to know that this man worked 40 or more hours a week. He worked different hours every week.

"Personally, is there anything you consider dangerous about social drinking?"

He said, "Not about 'responsible drinking.'"

He also said, "Addiction. There is *always a chance* of addiction."

I asked, "How would a person stay responsible about drinking?"

He said, "Read the danger signs such as being in trouble with the law, money problems, having bad thoughts about you and still drinking!"

His advice is, don't drink if you're in trouble with the law, have money problems, or feel bad about yourself.

**Here are three examples that he gave me of "being responsible":

A) "If you need to drive somewhere, ***don't*** drink!" (In my opinion, if you already had a drink and you need to go somewhere, take the bus, disability van, or a taxicab. Other possibilities are calling a friend to drive you or walk.)

B) "If you are angry, don't drink. ***Wait*** until your anger is gone. Alcohol will make your anger worse."

C) "If you feel bad about yourself, don't drink. Alcohol is a drug that makes a person feel sad."

He is now 70 years old and has not had a drink in 15-20 years. Why? Over the years alcohol has caused him headaches when he drank. He started drinking for social reasons at age 16. He just wanted to experiment and be cool by fitting in with his friends.

My next few questions are about how alcohol makes a person feel. "Personally, is there anything you consider enjoyable about social drinking?"

He said, "Yes."

"What is it?"

He said, "Releasing inhibitions and lightening of the spirit."

"Were there any sensations?"

He said, "Flying with the eagles and lightening of the spirit."

In talking with this man, I found out his job was stressful. He didn't get Saturday and Sunday off. He would come home from work usually on *his* Friday, sit down with one or two cans of beer before bedtime. He would sit alone, watch TV to relax. Once he relaxed, he'd go to bed! (He usually got two weekdays off, not the regular weekend days. He usually drank when he got home from working the swing shift!) (end)

These people should not drink:

- Pregnant women! If a pregnant woman drinks, the unborn baby is also getting the alcohol into his/her bloodstream.
- People under age 21. In most of the 50 states, you are breaking the law if you drink before you are 21 years old.
- People who are chemically dependent.

Look at all three of the recovering alcoholic interviews to find out why it is bad for people who are recovering to drink.

There are also people who choose to stay away from alcohol for health, religious, and personal reasons. (Alcohol Pamphlet)

People have different religious and personal beliefs. People also have different health issues and have to take different medicines so they might choose not to drink for health reasons.

It is dangerous to drink and drive. Drink OR drive. **_Never_** drink and drive at the same time!!

Are there dangers to social drinking? Yes! "Even one or two drinks slow down judgment and reaction time. So does a hangover." (Alcohol Pamphlet) One of my friends told me that one out of four social drinkers become an alcoholic.

The third interview is with a female age 30-40 years old. She has never taken a drink of alcohol except for communion at church.

I am going to start out with her childhood thoughts about alcohol. She thought all alcohol was bad and all people who drank alcohol were bad. She thought alcohol caused all people who drank to be abusive and mean. She didn't know the difference between light drinkers and heavy drinkers. She changed her mind!

As a teenager, she chose not to drink because she wanted to drive. She thought her parents would let her take driver's education if she made smart choices. She was wrong! They didn't!

Second, she thought drinking alcohol when you are underage is wrong. Her Christian belief was to obey the law and one of the laws says you must be 21 or older to legally drink. She asked a student pastor before she turned 21, "I am going to be 21 years old and feel that drinking is wrong, but I don't know why. What are your thoughts?" He said, "If it is not good for a child, then why is it good for an adult?" She liked the way he left her with something to think about instead of talking down to her. Why? He was nice and gave her facts. He did not react to her questions.

I was physically distant from my family members who were alcoholics and recovering alcoholics. I saw the results of two popular teenage boys three years after I made the choice to never legally drink. The boy I cared about dropped out of school after the 11th grade. The other boy turned to illegal drugs. I don't know anyone who got killed by a drunk driver.

At age 43, here is how I think through alcohol:

- I have different reasons why I avoid each of the following: liquor, beer, white wine, and red wine.
- I can get the same flavor or taste from liquor as I can from a nonalcoholic drink when I choose to drink.

- I have never drank beer! Every time I thought about drinking beer, I wanted to escape problems. That's the wrong reason to drink. I won't drink if it's for the wrong reason.
- I have heard that wine has medical benefits, so I did more research. I found out that there is white and red wine.

There's **no** research that white wine has medical benefits therefore I refuse to drink white wine!

Regarding red wine: This is the wine that people are referring to when they say alcohol is good for them medically. I did my personal research. Even if my doctor or pharmacist say drinking red wine is bad for me, I might drink red wine anyway, but I would only drink the recommended amount that a doctor says is the correct amount for health benefits! However, if drinking red wine is the only thing stopping me from getting my driver's license, **I won't drink!**

*Do your own research on alcohol!

*Don't trust my research alone!

I'm not an expert!

Why do people drink? "People may choose to drink for cultural, religious, medical, social or personal reasons...Most alcohol use is for social purposes, to relax at get-togethers or to celebrate an occasion. Some people use alcohol to forget worries for the moment or to escape reality." (Alcohol Pamphlet)

Drinking to forget or to escape reality is one of the warning signs that you are headed for trouble with alcohol and may lose control.

When I thought about being a light social drinker, I made the choice never to drink in a bar! Why? I don't enjoy visiting with people who have been drinking! No matter what my choice is I have to take responsibility for my choices! I did my own research and made my educated choice!

My fourth interview is with a female social drinker who is 30-40 years old. At age 14, she started to experiment with alcohol. When she became of legal age, the reason she chose to be a social drinker was for family and social gatherings. She also liked the buzz…the stepping out of herself. Later in life she decided she liked to be alone when she drank, so she only drank at home. She never drinks as a way to escape reality.

"Is there anything you consider enjoyable about social drinking?"

"Yes."

"What is it?"

"Looser feelings…stepping out."

"Is there anything you consider dangerous about social drinking?"

"Yes."

"What is it?"

"Choosing to drink and drive at the same time and becoming dependent or addicted to alcohol." She also believes in responsible drinking.

"Can people become dependent on alcohol?"

"Yes." (end)

Alcohol causes mental and physical dependence and can mess up your emotions real bad. (Alcohol Pamphlet)

"Dependence" means your mind and body thinks you need the alcohol and if you don't drink, you will suffer physically, mentally, and emotionally!

"When a drinker uses alcohol as an escape from problems and stress, and have come to depend on alcohol for relief, they have developed psychological or mental dependence on it. The more they drink, the more they think they need. The body requires more alcohol to function, and physical dependence has developed. Once, dependent, drinkers experience withdrawal symptoms when they stop drinking." (Alcohol Pamphlet)

My fifth interview was with a nondrinker! He is now 50-60 years old. At age 15, some friends stole some alcohol and they all drank it. They also broke the law in other ways that night. He got drunk twice with his buddies, and he got sick both times. His parents wanted him to get new friends. He didn't listen. He chose to join their group. After two times of getting drunk, he decided it was more fun "babysitting the drunks" by being the designated driver. Why? He thought it was more fun watching them act stupid and keeping all of them safe. He stopped being the designated driver when they asked him to do illegal drugs. Two of his friends died from alcoholism.

When he lived in California, he got drunk again once at a house, and got sick again. Just before his 21st birthday, he had to *force* one of his friends to quit drinking! If his friend didn't stop drinking, he **was going to die**! His friend knew he would die, but his friend could not stop drinking on *his* own! The man I interviewed made a choice at age 20, "If I never take another drink, I cannot become an alcoholic." Later in life, he met a lady who couldn't move from the neck down. Why? A drunk driver hit the car she was riding in! Her health got worse over the years, and she died a few years later.

An alcoholic is a person who has a drinking problem. Alcoholism is a disease. An alcoholic is a person who drinks and drinks and continues to drink even though bad things are happening. Alcoholics don't know *when* they have had enough or too much to drink. However, getting drunk over and over again is a warning sign of alcoholism! Alcohol CAN kill. "Most alcohol deaths are due to horrible injuries, illnesses and the organs in their body being damaged over the years because of drinking. Even light drinkers can die from respiratory failure after drinking a large amount of alcohol. Severe alcohol withdrawal can also cause death. When alcohol is combined with prescription and/or over- the-counter drugs, there's a higher chance of it killing them." (Alcohol Pamphlet)

The sixth person I interviewed is a female recovering alcoholic. She is between 50-59 years old. She started drinking at age 19 because it was socially acceptable. Her family drank and it was also in her family environment, therefore it is in her bloodstream. Since her family drank that is how she was taught to handle stress and that is called "environmental."

"Did you choose to stop drinking or were you forced to stop by the court system, by the Division of Developmental

Disabilities system, or by the Mental Health system?"

"I chose to quit."

"Why?"

"I was aware of what alcoholism was, so I set up some boundaries for myself that if I crossed those boundaries I would quit or get help to quit." When she chose to stop drinking, she realized that she had a chemical imbalance.

"How did you stop drinking?"

"First, I went to a couple of AA meetings, then to an inpatient treatment place for three months. When I got out of there, I went to AA meetings for one year and now I go only when I need to."

"Why did it take you so long before you chose to quit?"

"I reached my personal limit."

"How long did you drink?"

"At the time of the interview, I am not drinking." (However, before this book was put in print she did start drinking again.)

If someone becomes a recovering alcoholic, there's hope. However, life will be more difficult. It is possible for recovering alcoholics to go to school and keep a job. These things are easier to get and keep when a person realizes they have a drinking problem. It helps to change their ways when they are not being forced to change.

My seventh interview was with a male recovering alcoholic. He is 50-59 years old. He tried alcohol one time at age 5. He started drinking regularly at age 13. He and his friends broke the law by stealing alcohol and getting drunk.

"How long did you drink?"

"Twenty-three years."

"Why did you stop drinking?"

"At age 35 years old, my oldest daughter was born. I did not want her seeing or living in the environment of violence and anger caused by alcohol."

"Do your children have less of a chance of becoming an alcoholic because they were raised in an alcohol-free environment?"

"Yes, but my children still have a 'predisposition' to alcohol." ("Predisposition" means that a person is more likely to become an alcoholic if their birth family drinks or drank before he/she was born!)

"Did you choose to stop or were you forced to stop drinking?"

"I chose to."

"Why did you choose to quit?"

"(I quit) for my kids' sake."

"What took you so long before quitting?"

"I did not want to. I knew I had a problem, but I did not care."

"How long have you been sober?"

"Over 17 years."

"Any relapses?"

He said, "Not since I have been in AA."

"Does having a history of alcoholism make college or employment easy, difficult or make no difference?"

"The first five years of being sober was hard because I was setting new boundaries and had to make new friends. After five years of being sober, it was easier."

"Why after five years?"

"After five years, it was easier because I made new friends, who helped me stick to my new boundaries. I set for myself that alcohol is 100% off limits!"

"As an outsider looking in and having no experience, why do people think drinking is so fun?"

He said, "Fun, socialization, and partying...these are the main reasons. It also helps break up the boredom."

"What would you want me to say are the bad things?"

"Throwing up, hangovers, having sex with someone you don't even know, not caring about yourself...stop taking care of your hair, teeth, and body, and stop taking care of personal business along with stop caring about your family and friends. *Alcohol becomes the most important thing in an alcoholic's life!*"

"Is there any such thing as a 'responsible drinker'?"

"Yes, there is, absolutely!"

"Who can?"

"The person who has only one or two drinks or the person who stops drinking when they start feeling the effects of alcohol is a 'responsible drinker' and has no negative effects from drinking."

ALCOHOLICS CANNOT BE RESPONSIBLE DRINKERS!

"Did you need any supports personally or professionally when you quit?"

"Yes."

"What were they?"

"AA meetings, conferences, Dr. Milam, and reading the book, *Under the Influence*."

"Do you have any other comments?"

"The main reason teenagers choose to drink alcohol is peer pressure and wanting to fit in with the crowd. ***Think before*** you make choices because you will live with the results—good and bad!"

If you have a problem with alcohol, you can get help from a counselor or a treatment center. "In addition, research show the support of other recovering persons such as those in Alcoholics Anonymous can help people get sober and keep their sobriety." (Alcohol Pamphlet)

"If you suspect you have a drinking problem, you can get information and guidance from your medical doctor, your nearest drug treatment center, or mental health center. You can find these places in the phonebook by looking up 'Alcoholism,' 'Drug & Addiction Services,' 'Family Counselors,' or 'Mental Health Services' in the Yellow Pages." (Alcohol Pamphlet) You can also find support systems on the internet.

TO CHOICE MAKER: Now that you have some information from an alcohol pamphlet and have read seven interviews of how they made their choices and what the results were, you can make an educated choice.

If you still need more information, ask your support team, doctor, pharmacist, caregivers, people at your place of worship (if you have one), and close friends who care about you!

Here's a list of questions:

- Are you curious about alcohol?
- Are you afraid of the way alcohol would make you feel?
- Do you take prescription medicine? If you take prescription medicine, talk to your doctor or pharmacist.
- If you are in high school and want to drink, will coaches or music teachers let you play sports or be in music class if you smoke?
- Do you think there are health benefits to drinking alcohol?
- Have you done research on health benefits and health risks to drinking alcohol?
- Do you want to spend your money on alcohol?
- Is the possibility of becoming addicted to alcohol worth the risk of trying alcohol?
- Do you have religious beliefs about drinking?
- What do you know about drinking safely such as keeping yourself and the community safe while drinking?
- Have you had family members or friends killed by drunk drivers?
- Which is more important: drinking or driving?
- Do you know anyone who abuses alcohol?
- How do you think other drinkers behave?
- What is your value system?
- How are you going to protect yourself from addiction?
- How are you going to protect yourself from being a drunk driver?
- How are you going to stay safe while you are drinking and not fall into the wrong crowd?
- Finally, if you want to drink, why? State your reasons.

TO SUPPORT TEAM: I realize support teams have wisdom and that is why they have been chosen to be a part of the support team. However, he/she will never get the chance to learn new information and use it if they never get to ask the experts questions to make their own choices.

Sometimes, it's easier to respect someone's "forced choices" if/when the support team tells the choice maker how they made their choice about drinking! For example, did you or do you drink? If yes, why? If you quit, why? If you are a social drinker, how often do you drink? If you choose to avoid alcohol, why? What reasons do you have for your personal opinion about alcohol?

I would also suggest answering the same set of questions *with them* before they have answered them. Tell them if they have a predisposition to alcohol. If so, how many relatives are addicted?

TO BOTH OF YOU: Alcohol is a serious topic! When talking to each other, **listen** *to each other*!

It is very important for each of you to understand why you have the opinion you have.

Illegal Drugs

I never considered taking illegal drugs. Why? It's against the law. I'm a person who always follows the rules. As long as illegal drugs are against the law, I won't take them. Second, I take prescription medicines. I don't want to take anything I don't have to.

Over-the-counter medicines are legal. However, always talk to *your* pharmacist about every over-the-counter medicine before taking it. They know what over-the-counter medicines work best with the medicines you take.

How can you know if a drug is legal? Legal drugs are medicines that doctors prescribe and that you pick up at the pharmacy or that can be bought at any store that sells them.

The only reason I am writing anything about illegal drugs is, there are bad people out in the world, and they might ask you to take illegal drugs. If your goal is to ride the city bus or if you want to live on your own, you need to learn how to say, "NO," and when to say, "NO!"

I was shocked to find out that most illegal drugs have the *same dangers*! I thought the dangers would be different for each one! I got my information from pamphlets, TV, and from talking to recovering drug addicts.

A possible benefit or reward of avoiding illegal drugs is getting financial aid if you choose to go to college! People who want to be in the military must have avoided illegal drugs!

Illegal drugs affect every user differently! Users will probably not get every side effect, but they cannot choose which side effects they will get and which ones they won't!

Illegal drugs cause the body and the brain to be damaged.

- If a person uses drugs, they could get heart failure or an increased heart rate.
- A user can have trouble breathing, breathe too fast or their lungs could fail and they will die.
- Users risk kidney problems or failure.
- Most illegal drugs can give users increased blood pressure.
- I read about one illegal drug that can lower blood pressure.
- A person who uses illegal drugs could get hepatitis or AIDS from sharing needles. Dirty needles increase the danger of getting AIDS or hepatitis. If you get AIDS, you will *eventually* die! There is no cure for AIDS or HIV!
- A user may get sick more often from colds, flu's, viruses, or diseases than people who avoid drugs.
- People who use illegal drugs can have drug related brain seizures that can kill quickly.

Epileptic seizures are different than a seizure from a drug

44

overdose. Epilepsy and seizure disorders are different! Talk to *your* doctor if you have questions!

- There are some illegal drugs that, if taken, can possibly make you lose the desire to eat.
- It's possible to vomit over and over.
- It's possible to feel like you are going to faint.
- There are some illegal drugs out there that the user takes to keep them awake when they want to sleep.
- There are others that put the user to sleep. (Michael Jackson used illegal drugs to get some sleep. He died because of it!)
- A user might lose their balance or stumble.
- Blurred vision from illegal drug use can cause headaches.
- A user's muscles could ache.
- They could have pain in their face from grinding their teeth together without realizing it.
- They could have trouble concentrating.
- A user might have long-term or short-term memory problems or have no memory at all.
- Some illegal drugs cause a user to forget what they did while under the influence. Even if you don't remember breaking the law, you are still responsible for your actions. That could include jail/prison or fines.

*I have met three people with memory problems.

With most illegal drugs, users build up a tolerance causing the (real or imagined) need to take more and more illegal drug(s) to get the same high. This is called a physical addiction!

- A user can lose their awareness of touch and pain. They can put their hand on a hot stove without feeling any pain. They would not know their hand was on a hot stove unless they saw it!
- A user may have to pee or poop more often or have constipation.

- A user might get a skin rash.
- If illegal drugs are taken through the nose (snorted), damage to the nose can be for life. There is nothing doctors can do to fix the damage snorting causes!
- A user can get a fever.
- A user may lose concern for their health by not eating or sleeping.
- A user can have problems with slurred speech or the words may be clear, but the sentences might not make sense to the listener.
- A coma is possible and can be deadly.
- One illegal drug I read about can *kill* a user from taking that illegal drug one time!

Here are the dangers to your emotions, self-control, and mind. (The following side effects can be symptoms of a mental illness or side effects from taking illegal drugs. If a person already has a mental illness and they use illegal drugs, their symptoms can be much worse. Some people get a mental illness because of taking illegal drugs. Mental illness is another disability. There are people who have mental illnesses who have never taken illegal drugs!)

- Users can lose some of their emotional control.
- Users can get depression.
- Users can just lose control.
- Users can have anxiety attacks, panic attacks, or paranoia.
- Users can become very suspicious.
- Users can become confused.
- Users can have flashbacks.
- Users can be more irritable.
- Users might lose interest in food, family, friends, and other activities.
- Users might have a sense of distance or estrangement.
- Illegal drugs might over stimulate the nervous system.

- Users can have delusions or hallucinations.
- Users can get a false view of reality!
- Illegal drug use can cause schizophrenic-psychosis behavior.
- Users can get schizophrenia that lasts a lifetime. *There are people who have schizophrenia who have never taken illegal drugs!*
- Users can get chronic/constant psychosis from illegal drug use.
- Users can get toxic psychosis.
- Users can have violent behavior and be involved in bizarre accidents or violent crimes including murders.
- Illegal drugs can impair your judgment!
- Illegal drugs might slow down the mental processing system!
- Users might forget who they were before taking drugs.
- Illegal drugs may cause "catatonic symptoms." Catatonic means the person becomes unable to talk, lethargic, disoriented (confused about their surroundings), and makes meaningless movements or any combination of the four.
- Users may forget what it was like to live life without taking illegal drugs.
- *If a user feels the need to take illegal drugs every day, they are addicted physically and mentally.
- If a user continues to use illegal drugs while taking prescription drug(s), the user will probably have more severe symptoms!
- If the user drinks alcohol and takes illegal drugs, their symptoms will probably be much worse!

Doctors went to school to learn how to make people well! Pharmacists went to school to learn how all drugs work together! If you don't tell your doctor and pharmacist everything they ask you, they can't help you. If you have two or more doctors prescribing you medicines, ***tell every doctor and pharmacist about every medicine you take***!!

- If a woman is pregnant and uses illegal drugs, she might have a miscarriage/stillborn baby.
- A woman who is pregnant and using illegal drugs can also deliver a child with severe disabilities.

Users don't have money! The reasons are:

1) A user has a hard time keeping a job because they have problems showing up on time for work or they forget to show up for work.
2) Illegal drugs are very, very expensive. They are so expensive that users eventually stop paying their rent/house, electricity bill, the phone bill, and stop buying food. Why? They'd rather buy drugs than pay the bills.

One of my Christian friends stayed off drugs for years and he died about a year ago when he was offered drugs again ***and took the offer***!

Please don't!!

Finally, doing illegal drugs puts users at risk of losing:

- Family
- Friends
- Job
- Health
- Faith/religion!

Why? Illegal drugs become the most important thing in a user's life!

Therefore, for the protection of your physical, emotional, social, mental, and possibly spiritual health, I won't give anyone the choice of taking illegal drugs!

The number one concern I would have would be losing my freedom by being in prison!

Learning How to Budget Your Money

I approach the subject of money with caution. It is very easy to spend all the money you have and still need more. Therefore, think carefully where and when you spend your money.

A budget is a plan that shows you how you will use your money.

I have been managing my own money for 21 years. When I was single, I never signed a contract unless my parents said it was ok! Now that I'm married, I won't sign a contract unless my husband says it's okay. That's my personal choice too!

If the people you trust tell you that signing something is a *bad idea*, **don't sign it**! However, find out why, but not in front of the salesperson!

Here's a list of things my parents, the church, or a disability agency taught me about budgeting money. My parents have always been great at budgeting money and they were great at teaching me how to budget my money. They taught me by giving me an allowance and by paying me for the chores I did around the house. They also taught me how to save money and to spend it wisely!

As I grew older, my parents said they would give $10 to a store for every $1 that I gave the store toward a new bedroom set. I still have most of my bedroom set today. (I bought a new bed six years ago.) I believe my parents and I started buying the original bedroom set while I was in the third grade and I made the final payment when I finished the sixth grade.

My parents did this for three reasons:

A) To teach me budgeting skills.
B) They didn't know what my future husband's budgeting skills would be.
C) They also knew that most people live paycheck-to-paycheck. My parents were not rich, but they knew how to pay their bills off quickly so they could buy more

things and avoid paying more interest than was necessary.

A disability agency that teaches independent living skills also taught me how to budget money while getting a government check. The disability agency realized I had a higher level of budgeting skills than most people they serve and that what I needed to learn was totally different. My needs included: Needing to know what questions to ask a salesperson, how to know if a price was reasonable, and when to buy something that's on sale.

They taught me to ask myself the following four questions to find out if the product or service that's on sale is something I should buy at the time of the sale:

1) Are all my bills paid?
2) Can I afford it?
3) How often will I use the product or service?
4) Can I wait for the next sale?

Ask yourself the four questions above to decide if what's on sale is a good deal *for you or will you use it*! If you are not going to use a product very often and you need it, can you borrow it instead of buying it or will you use it enough times to make it worth the price?

Here is something I bought at a garage sale—a blue vase.

1) Yes, all my bills were paid.
2) Yes, I needed it because I had caught a bride's bouquet and I had nothing to put the bouquet in. The vase was blue and a perfect match for the bouquet.
3) Yes, I wanted it, and yes, it would be used.

Therefore, *it was a good sale for me*!

Because I started learning how to budget money at a very young age, I never needed a payee!

The basics of budgeting your money are to pay your bills first, then you can do what you want with the rest of your money.

"Required bills" means bills that you **must pay**! There are five! The first is rent/mortgage! You must have a place to live, but it's your choice what kind of place you live in. The second required bill that must be paid every month is the electricity bill. The third required bill is a telephone.

The fourth required bill is buying enough food for yourself, so you don't run out before your next paycheck comes. The funny thing about buying food is that no bill shows up in the mailbox saying you owe this much money. You have to figure out how much to spend. How? (A) How much do you eat a day, a week, a month and (B) what stores do you shop at? This includes discount food stores or grocery stores. Don't include eating at restaurants.

The fifth required bill is transportation. The cheapest transportation is walking and riding a bike. If you don't want to walk or ride a bike all over town, you need money to ride the city bus, the disability van, or drive. The next chapter talks about transportation.

Remember these were *my* choices and *my* opinions! I am responsible for *my choices* whether my choices are good or bad!

*Make your own choices! However, if you don't like the results of your choices, make different choices *in the future*!

Handling Your Money

There are different ways to handle money. The most common way is with a **checking account**. The bank or credit union gives you a little booklet called a registry to write down every time you deposit or withdraw money from your account.

Deposit means putting money into your account.

Withdrawal means taking money out of your account such as when you pay your bills. You write a check when you withdraw or take money out of your account. A check is a small piece of paper that is a form of money. When it is filled out, you must write down:

- Who gets the money
- How much money they get
- The date you wrote the check
- Sign it

If you can't remember to write down every time you deposit or withdraw money from your account, you'll never know how much money you have! Why? Money doesn't come out of a checking account until someone cashes the check! It would be smart to get a different type of account! I know I forget to write everything down, so I will never get a checking account. I need my money put in or taken out of my account immediately!

A **debit card** is a different way to pay your bills and buy things. A debit card is the same size card as a State ID card. A debit card won't let you spend more money than you have in your account. If you are interested in a debit card, call the bank or credit union and ask them. Most people choose to get a debit card. Why? It takes the money immediately out of your account and you don't have to stand there while you are filling out a check. You don't have to wait for the business to cash the check. The business has their money and you know how much you have left!

Saving Money

A **savings account** is an account with a bank or a credit union. You deposit money into the account and usually don't withdraw it until there's enough money to buy an expensive item such as an HD TV. Money can also be taken out when there's an emergency such as needing to repair the dishwasher.

I strongly believe in saving money. By saving money and looking for a good deal on Bibles, my friend was able to buy four leather Bibles for the four criminals that hurt his daughter.

If my friend had spent all his money instead of saving some of it, he could not have bought the Bibles. (He chose to buy them Bibles instead of hating them because hating them would not undo the damage.)

Money orders are like checks that you buy but the difference is that the money you're spending is in your account! Personally, I'd rather pay for things by money order or cash instead of having a protective payee or taking the chance of bouncing a check by writing a check and discovering the money was not in my account. **Bouncing a check is also called an overdraft.**

The price of one overdraft charge can be more expensive than the money order fees and the cost of a protective payee for one month. When I started paying my own bills, money orders were cheaper.

Credit unions and banks have _different rules_. A credit union is run by its members. A bank is in business to make money.

My parents had an account at a credit union for many years, so I opened my savings account there. My parents chose to leave the credit union; however, the credit union is still a good place to do business. People sometimes choose to change where they do business for different reasons. Examples of why people change where they do business:

- Better prices
- The customer or business moves
- Another business offers something you need that the other business didn't offer

At age 16, I started going to a different church that teaches giving some money to God. I didn't start giving money to God until I was 23 years old.

Credit Cards

Using a credit card is a form of borrowing money. It's borrowing from a bank or a credit union. Anything that you charge on a credit card **must be paid back!** IF a person does not pay their credit card bill, the bank or credit union will take the credit card away, and the money will still have to be paid back.

My parents only told me that credit cards were bad, but they never told me why. I wanted to find out if there were good reasons for owning a credit card *before* I made my choice. I chose to get one! When I got one credit card, I chose to get it, and I chose *carefully when to use it*! I only use it once in a while!

After researching credit cards, my **personal** opinion is that credit cards are good for emergencies and going on vacation. Sometimes, I buy something on the credit card when I don't have any cash in my purse. I use my credit card and next time I go to the credit union I pay the credit card bill. Sometimes, I pay the bill before it shows up in the mailbox.

If you learn how to manage and budget your savings and checking account, it *might be* safe to get one credit card! If you need or want a credit card, learn the credit card language and what each word means. Ask your support team.

When I was thinking of making an expensive purchase on my credit card, I took a friend with me to protect me financially. One of my purchases was a recliner for our 20 year old son! After we paid off the recliner, I wanted to buy a living room set to match the recliner! I paid the bill off quickly!

Traveler's checks can be tracked. Tracked means they can be found by an identification number. People use traveler's checks when they travel out of town.

Gambling

Gambling is stupid (author's opinion)! (I don't know how to explain it. Ask your support team.) Television makes it look wonderful. It's not! When I was 12 or 13 years old, I was interested in gambling. My mom said gambling was a waste of money. She said, "Gambling is like throwing your money away."

Finally, one day when I was about 15 years old, she found a winning ticket worth $2 that someone had thrown on the ground. She picked it up and gave me the choice to keep the cash or to buy two more tickets. If we won any money, the money would be mine. I chose to buy two more tickets. We lost the $2. My mom said, "If we had just cashed in the ticket, you would have been $2 richer."

I decided mom might be right, but I had to ask some people in my church before I made my final decision. The people at church and my mom told me that there's a better chance of losing money. A few people win, but most people lose. If you lose, you also lose the money that you spent to buy the tickets. So, in my early 20's, I decided gambling was a waste of money. I've made a choice to never gamble! (I've only gambled one time as an adult!) Gambling to me is foolish, but is not against my religious or health beliefs, etc.

Lending Money to Friends

I was taught that if I give money to friends or strangers, they would want to be my friend only for my money and strangers might see me as an easy target.

I have lent money to friends when I lacked the judgment of what was a need and what was a want! However, my bills *were always paid* **when** I loaned the money! In one case, it was hard to get my money back because my friend's protective payee was unwilling to pay me back. I finally did get paid back! How? I talked to the payee's coworker.

I wanted the payee to know that it was his client's idea to pay me back. I got paid back, but the payee gave my friend a very hard time for it. He forced his personal opinion on his client.

Character means you know a person by how they behave and what they say and do or don't say and do.

There are also some family members who try to force their values on people who have a protective payee. It is illegal for someone to force you to accept their values! However, it's legal and healthy to share your values with others and for others to share their values with you!

*The situation with that payee has taught me to never lend money to anyone who has a protective payee. It's okay to give money to someone who has a payee, but to never lend it because *I won't* get it ***if I need it***!*

Borrowing Money

Borrowing is the opposite of lending. Borrowing is very bad. Why? Any time a person borrows money they are in debt! If you borrow money from a friend and they need the money back at a time when you are unable to pay your friend back, that's unfair to your friend!

If you need money, it is best to borrow it from a bank or credit union. Banks and credit unions charge money for lending money to customers. The charge for borrowing their money is called interest. (Ask your support team what interest is.)

The main reason people get a loan is to buy very expensive things such as a house or to go to college. Loan is a different word for borrowing money. A person or agency that lends the money gives the borrower a loan. Banks or credit unions usually give loans based on how much money a person makes (and other reasons) so the lender can decide whether the borrower is financially able to pay them back.

Giving Money to People

I gave money to a friend once in the form of paying her phone bill! I only did this once! I paid her phone bill for four reasons.

A) Since we talk to each other daily for hours at a time, we wouldn't have been able to talk to each other for a few months!
B) My friend was very, very responsible with money, but she got into trouble one month. I gave it as a gift and not as a loan.
C) She did not ask me! She's paid her bills every month since I paid her phone bill. That was over five years ago.
D) All my bills *were paid* at the time. I **chose** to pay her bill!

Paying my bills every month is why I don't have a protective payee! A payee *can be* helpful for some people. Getting your bills paid needs to be your basic rule!

There are bills that are optional. Optional bills in this book mean things you have or want, but you can live without even if you are addicted to it.

Below is a true story which explains why it's very important to know who your real friends are!

My second ex-fiancé had invited his friend into my apartment and I wanted him to leave and never come back! I knew him from middle school and high school, and he made me feel unsafe. I distrusted him and did not want to find out why. My fiancé insisted he stay, so I let the guy in.

Here's what happened: I set money aside to give to church. While I was in the bathroom, he stole it. I told the thief he stole money I was giving to the church! I told him, that was God's money and it was between God and him! The point: Choose your friends wisely!

He took advantage of the situation. Taking financial advantage means stealing money, personal property, or borrowing money with no plan of paying the person back! This would be using someone for your own financial gain without caring how it affects the other person.

I told my ex-fiancé to choose between that thief and me, and he chose the thief because he hated confrontation!

By choosing to never let that man in my apartment again, I set a boundary that protected my property! The above example is what I mean by explaining to your support team *why* you want or don't want someone to be your friend.

Some people want to own a home instead of renting or want to own a car. Both of these are very expensive because of the cost of maintenance, insurance, gas, etc. Everybody has to save their money for the things they want in life!

Are you paying all your required bills before your optional bills? Most people say they can't live without a television, so they have cable or dish no matter how expensive it is.

If you believe in giving, you will want to write it down as a bill. It may go to a religious place or a nonprofit organization like The Arc. The rest of your money is your money! Money you may save or spend! If you don't have enough money, get a job.

I have the attitude that you *never stop learning* no matter who you are! It doesn't matter if a person has the worst disability you've ever seen or if a person is the smartest person ever, everyone learns every day! No one is perfect, so when someone makes a mistake it's an opportunity for them to learn from their mistake(s) through *natural consequences*! Don't protect others from natural consequences.

It is important enough to say again: Be careful who your friends are, especially if managing your money is your goal.

Ask yourself the following questions:

- How often is a friend around when you don't have any money?
- How often does a friend pay for them self when the two of you are together?
- How often do they ask you to pay for them?

- Do they ever offer to pay for you?
- Ask yourself the above questions about ten times for each person.

Talk to your support team about your answers, and then decide if you want to keep each person as a friend.

A reason I was able to lend or give money to a friend was I had a job and my life was (and still is) God-centered.

Before I help someone financially, I see if they have asked every government agency and religious organization to help them financially before I will think about helping them. If they didn't ask, I'd tell them to ask all of them first. If they asked and all the organizations said "no," I'd find out why they said no. Depending on their reasons for saying no and how many times they've asked me to help them out and depending on why they are asking for the money helps me decide if I will help them!

You may have realized that the world revolves around money. You have to give money to a business to receive a service or product. For example, you give money to the bus company to receive a bus ride or a bus pass. Nothing is free.

TO CHOICE MAKER:

- Do you see how the way you live and who you hang out with matters when it comes to protecting your money?
- What would happen if you couldn't pay your required bills because someone stole your money?
- What would you do if your hobbies cost more than you earn every month?
- How important is it *to you* to pay for a place to live, electricity, one phone, a bus pass or have money for the bus or van and food if and when your food stamps run out for the month?

If you can manage your own money, you can buy things on sale, so you spend less for things you need and want.

Ask questions like:

- How much money do I get a month?
- What are my required bills?
- How much does each bill cost?
- How much money is left after my required bills are paid?

The leftover amount is your spending money. Even if you choose to add a second phone, cable/dish, etc., they're not required bills, but if you buy those services, it becomes a required bill you must pay, and it reduces your spending money.

TO SUPPORT TEAM: Always, listen to the choice maker's frustrations. Explain to them why you make the choices *you* make with their money. Tell them your own money mistakes and the consequences you have suffered. If you let your family and friends know what mistakes you have made with your own money, they probably won't feel as frustrated at the time.

An example, the choice maker might take some of your ideas, think about other ideas, and ignore some of your ideas. Instead of telling them something is too expensive, take them to the store, shop around for that item such as a cell phone with the understanding that you won't buy anything *at this time*, **but maybe at a later time**. Have them show you the phones they are interested in, and you show them the prices. Have the salesperson talk to **both of you** and explain all the possible monthly plans. When the two of you leave, ask and answer each other's questions.

Your goal: find out how much they knew before going to the store and learned after going to the store! This rule should apply no matter what the subject is. They might be better prepared next time they go shopping. It is the same process for every new thing they need or want to buy. This process could also be used to seek information.

TO BOTH OF YOU: If the choice maker has gotten into trouble with gambling, credit cards, etc., there are support groups and classes in the community to teach or re-teach money management skills. The support groups should be helpful. Regaining control of your money and **patiently** continuing to teach them may be the answer. If you have trouble with checks, checking accounts, credit cards, and/or buying things online, consider paying your bills with money orders, and avoid credit cards and buying things online!

Local Transportation

If you are low on money or want to exercise, you can walk, run, or ride a bike. There are three other possible ways to get around town:

A) Disability van
B) City bus
C) Driving

Disability Van

The disability van is one kind of public transportation. The only people allowed to ride the disability van are people who are eligible, their caregivers and their friends.

You must fill out paperwork to find out if you can ride the disability van. The transportation agency will send you a letter telling you if you are eligible. If you disagree with their decision, you have the right to challenge the decision, and you have the right to have someone with you when you challenge them.

Riding the van is much slower than riding the bus or driving! Why? The people who schedule the rides make too many rides. Why? They don't hire enough drivers and don't have enough vans.

The van is very safe. If you are physically challenged and can easily break a bone by falling or if you get easily confused, the van is the safest option! Why? The driver takes the passenger to the door, so riders never get lost!

The reason the van is my least favorite transportation is, I've been dropped off so early the doors were still locked. I was waiting all alone, and that was scary. Being dropped off late was just as bad when I was going to school, work, or especially to a doctor's appointment.

The third problem I've had is waiting up to 30 minutes or longer for them to pick me up. I have learned to deal with waiting by bringing things to do. I use my time wisely by calling doctors' offices, scheduling more van rides, doing my homework, etc. so when I get home, I can spend time doing whatever I want such as being with my family, resting, etc.

The van rules are different in every city and every State. In my city, this is how to set up rides. The rider or the caregiver needs to call and schedule a ride 2-7 days in advance. The schedulers need to have the rider's ID/identification number, the exact address of where they are going, the time they want to be picked up, and the exact time they need to be there if they have an appointment. The rider has to give them 75-90 minutes to get there on time!

If you live on your own, you must schedule your own van rides!

Riding the City Bus

The city bus is another kind of public transportation. A lot of people without disabilities ride the bus for many reasons. Here are some of the reasons:

- Driving is expensive
- They lost their driver's license
- It's good for the environment

Different types of people ride the city bus. They include:

- People of different social and economic backgrounds
- People of different educational and professional backgrounds
- People of different races
- People of different ages
- People of different genders
- People of different religious and political backgrounds
- People with and without disabilities
- People who are homeless

You need to know how to keep yourself safe if you ride the city bus! Here are some ideas:

1) Be aware of who and what is around you.
2) Know the bus routes.
3) Do not make eye contact or talk to other passengers until you know how to safely ask for help.
4) Be aware of the people around you—their clothes, height, weight, and everything else that identifies a person.
5) If and when you see or hear trouble, report it to a worker.
6) When you are learning who is safe to talk to on the bus, only talk to people you trust from your place of worship, work or school. As you learn, you can talk to more people.

When I moved out of my parent's home and rented a room, the first thing I did was ride every city bus multiple times. I did this because I didn't know the streets well enough to understand the bus schedules and maps. (I also have trouble with maps.) At that time, I had no responsibilities.

My social experience was extremely limited. Since I was so sheltered growing up, I did not know how to tell if someone was safe.

TO CHOICE MAKER: Do you want to learn or relearn how to ride the city bus? What would you do if they change the bus routes?

1) If you are eligible, ride the disability van until you learn how to get to the place you are going. If the route changes, go back to the van until you relearn it. For example, you might only know the bus to get to work. Take the bus to and from work, and ride the van everywhere else until you know how to get somewhere else, etc.
2) Ask the bus company which bus goes to the address you want to go to?

3) Find out if the place you are going is on the street the bus drops you off on or if you have to walk a block or more.

4) Ask the driver to tell you when he/she gets to your stop. If you have to walk a few blocks, ask the driver to point you in the right direction and take the disability van home until you learn how to get home from where you are!

5) If you continue to have trouble learning the buses and you still want to learn to ride, ask the bus company for special training!

6) Your support team can help you practice everything the bus company teaches you!

7) Tell the transportation company what your transportation needs are by going to transportation meetings, and by writing, calling, and emailing the administrators of the company. The administrators are who have control over the van and bus money. If we never tell them our transportation needs, they will spend the money how they think it will best serve us, instead of how it will _really help us_!

Finally, if you have tried everything and it does not work, I would strongly suggest staying on the disability van. However, it is your choice.

TO SUPPORT TEAM: The choice maker should slowly build his/her bus knowledge and apply the knowledge while riding the city bus and then gain more knowledge and apply that knowledge and repeat the process until you feel that they can ride the city bus alone.

TO BOTH OF YOU: _Everyone needs to learn to protect themselves,_ just in case someone tries to hurt them. You can protect yourself by using your voice, hands, pepper spray, a cell phone, etc. in an emergency.

Make sure you understand each other's boundaries so you can work together as a team! You must know what each other's needs and wants are so you can understand and communicate with each other.

Driving

Driving is the fastest way to get around town!

Driving is the only thing I still want to do that my parents still don't approve of!

When I entered 10th grade, I signed up for driver's education. After it was too late to drop classes, I had a seizure in class and the school pulled me out of driver's ed. and put me in study hall. I was so angry at both my parents and the school because they knew I had seizures. I begged my mom to keep my seizures *a secret*! My seizures were **mild**! The only time I ever blacked out was when I got very sick in the 3rd grade for seven days straight. I thought I could safely drive because I could feel my seizures coming on, I can carry on a conversation while having a seizure and have full use of the right side of my body while I'd have a seizure, so I'd be able to pull over or stop.

As of March 2011, only 30% of me still wanted to drive. Why? As of 2013, I only wanted to drive 5% of the time.

Some personal reasons: I was almost in a horrible car accident that I would not have been able to prevent. The other driver would have been at fault, but my driver was able to avoid it!

Financial/money reasons: It cost too much!

In February and March of 2011, I had three seizures I remember having **after** the seizure was done. However, I felt it coming on but was not alert during the seizure!

For people who have physical limitations, there are accommodations for driving. My parents were still against me driving. My dad believed in doing things the normal way and if it could not be done the normal way, it shouldn't be done at all. When I was 18 years old, my dad let me drive the truck in a field and I ran into a bale of hay. In my defense, I had no idea what the rules of the road were. I hadn't studied the driver's guide. The only thing I knew about driving is what I saw my parents doing.

When I was 25 or 26, my doctor gave me permission to learn to drive. Even though I was 7-8 years older and I had MY doctor's permission, my parents were still holding onto the bale of hay situation. They continued to hold that against me. When I told my parents that I did tell the doctor about being able to feel my seizures coming on they said, "That doctor must be a pretty stupid doctor to give you permission to drive."

I had four learner's permits. While I had my learner's permits, the Department of Vocational Rehabilitation said they would pay for me to learn to drive **if** I:

- Got a driver's license
- Bought a car or a truck
- Got insurance
- Could pay to fix the vehicle when it broke down

I got a new doctor to say it was okay for me to drive. Why? My old doctor wasn't my doctor any longer.

The reason the Department of Vocational Rehabilitation was willing to pay for my driver's education was people who can drive and who have a car have a better chance of finding a job. What frustrated me most was there was nothing I could do to show my parents that I would be a better driver than I was 7-8 years ago.

I thought they should at least tell me what I needed to do for me to earn their trust with their car! They refused to tell me. To them, it was a matter of, "We don't want you to!" The more my dad said, "You can't do it," the more I wanted to!

I chose to try another way of showing my dad it would be a good idea for me to drive. I started to tell my dad every time a drunk man walked up to me downtown or on the bus and made me feel very uncomfortable!

To make matters worse for my parents, in 1994, I got

interested in watching live shows. Most of them were at nighttime. There was a professional who enjoyed this music, and drove, and was unable to transport me. My parents disliked it.

I told my dad, 'Well, if you teach me how to drive, I would be safer when I go out at night."

Dad held his ground. "No!" Mom was quietly against it. Going to live shows was a requirement of a college class I was taking, so my dad told me to take that person with me to the shows. Why? He trusted (and still trusts) most of my judgment regarding people. He knew I would never get into a car with someone who drank too much alcohol or a stranger.

I had also tried taking the disability van. Sometimes, I would get there too early and sometimes, I would get there too late. Sometimes, I would have to wait for the disability van outside in the dark in the middle of downtown.

So, my dad and I would argue again about me driving. I tried using the statement, "You work swing shift. How dare you try to confine me to my apartment at night just because you don't want me to drive for your own peace of mind!"

I never had a safe place to practice driving. Finally, what helped me realize I could not drive (at that time) is a man named Eli let me try to steer his pedal car. It had four seats. He let me drive the pedal car, so if I had trouble steering, he could keep it on the road, and there would be less chance of crashing. The dream of driving took 20 years to die.

TO CHOICE MAKER: The reason I shared this failed goal and dream is to show that nobody gets everything they want in life. Try hard to get as independent as you can, but be realistic! Being independent means doing as much as you can for yourself, knowing when to ask questions and when to ask for help.

TO SUPPORT TEAM: The reason it took me so long to realize that I could not drive is that my parents refused to let me find out for myself how safe or dangerous it would be for me to drive. After my doctor gave me permission and I got my learner's permit, the Department of Vocational Rehabilitation said they would pay for my driver's education if I had a car and a desire to get a job! My parents had the ability to support me by letting me practice my driving lessons with their car.

Another reason I fought so hard for so long about my *perceived* right to drive is I had been told for so long that I couldn't do many things because of my many disabilities. I found out I could do almost everything I put my mind to with God's help. I proved to my parents that anything is possible! I now know driving isn't a right! If someone gets caught drinking and driving, they <u>*should lose*</u> their driver's license for life. If someone does something wrong because of their disability, they should be given chances and/or forced to take classes to help them do things safely with their disability.

Some people resent being told "no" when they don't understand why they can't do something. Letting the person with a disability find out they can't do something helps them learn what their limitations are. This can sometimes help them to say no on their own and will teach them when to say no. Help them figure out their limitations (including their financial limitations) by asking them specific questions just like you would with your other children!

If you make them part of the decision-making process, it will help you both in the future to get what you both need and want. This will help them gain the skills to make an informed choice. The goal should be:

- To teach them when to stand up for themselves
- To know when to ask questions
- To know when to accept someone else's answer

Learning a Job or a Career

A job or career is how people make money. However, the job must be learned before the work can be done. College helps people earn a higher paying job. A relative, friend, or someone you know can teach you how to do a job. Sometimes the boss teaches the employee what they want them to know and how they want the job done. This is called On the Job Training or OJT. There are also people who have a job coach that help them learn their job and help them keep their job.

School or College

I graduated from high school with a diploma. I took one year off from school, moved back to the city, and started college.

When I started college, I had to take classes below college level before I started taking regular classes. Below college level means classes below the 100 level. Examples of this would be writing 98, math 99, reading 97, etc. College level classes are the 100 level and above.

The first two years of college can be done at a community college, which is cheaper than a four-year college.

I took breaks in between college quarters a couple of times for different reasons. Some good reasons to take a temporary break(s) from school is:

- If college is causing you to have physical, mental, or emotional problems, finish the quarter or semester, then take a break before going back! Your health is more important than a college degree!
- Family Emergency
- Can't afford it

When a person goes to college, they are being trained to do a job with the hope of making more money in the future.

Examples of jobs that need a college degree are: doctors, pilots, lawyers, etc. There are a lot of jobs that require a college degree. If you want to go to college but you don't know what you want your lifetime career to be, take all the required classes for an AA degree. Once you know what you want to do, you can start taking the classes for that career.

Only take classes that the school counselor says you need and choose elective classes you want to take. Don't take college classes or get a degree that someone else wants you to. Take what you need and want! You might want a job you don't like so you can earn more money.

My College Choices

My first choice was taking the Early Childhood Education program. I chose this because I had been a teacher's aide for a semester, and the following year I was a Sunday school teacher's aide for a Sunday school class. Shortly after leaving the ministry, I started working at Ogden Hall as a teacher's aide.

While at school, the teacher handed me a pair of latex gloves. I started to put them on using my teeth. He said I couldn't use my teeth. I explained my disability. After a few more talks, they got me out of my classes. It was explained that state law requires that _all_ childcare workers must wear gloves. At that time, I didn't understand why all of my suggestions were unreasonable accommodations as long as the work got done and as long as I wasn't using my disability to avoid doing any part of the job that I could do! For example, let's say a person can't do something because their disability makes it impossible to do, then accommodate it. However, if someone uses their disability as a reason to avoid doing the job, then they should be fired!

I was frustrated and I didn't know what I wanted to do, so I dropped out of school for a few years. I didn't want to do anything education or employment related, but I stayed busy!

71

I finally decided I wanted to be a voice teacher. As I started my studies in music, I found out that I had to be able to play one other instrument besides my voice. After taking a few classes, I chose to drop out because most instruments require two hands. I thought it would be unfair to my students because I had to play an instrument with one hand and my students needed to learn to play correctly with two hands!

Next, I started listening to people who had mental health issues and intellectual disabilities. Most of them seemed very unhappy to have a guardian, protective payee and a caregiver because they wanted to do things their guardian, protective payee or caregiver would not let them do.

Later, I joined a Bible Study with people who had severe intellectual disabilities. Most of these people were unable to talk, unable to use their hands and unable to walk. However, they all had smiles on their faces and loved Jesus Christ. This made this group of people wonderful to be around. After two years of knowing them, I started hanging out with some of them outside the Bible Study.

This was hard on me because the people working in the helping profession overprotected them! What I mean by overprotecting is that most care giving agencies protect their clients from everyone who is not a professional. It seems reasonable to me to do a police background check on everyone who wants to be their friend and everyone the choice maker chooses as friends.

Another type of overprotecting is protecting people from doing things that are age appropriate.

When I found out that the problem of overprotecting and not listening to the people who have mental health issues and intellectual disabilities was a system-wide problem and not an agency problem, and that every agency seemed to be unable to change their policies to be more client friendly, I chose to go back to college and get my AA degree in social work! A social worker can work with many different groups of people. They can work with the elderly, children, or people who have intellectual disabilities and/or mental illnesses, etc.

Over the years, many people with intellectual disabilities have asked me to help them do different things or they tell me. Like, "My guardian won't let me _____ (fill in the blank)." I have continued to listen and ask questions like:

- "Why do you want to do that?"
- "Why won't they let you?"

I chose to write this book so I'd be able to help more people and teach them to do the things they were asking me to help them do. With this book and the workbook I wrote, I can put a class together to teach people the skills they need to learn so they can do the things they want to do.

TO CHOICE MAKER: How to decide if you want to go to college:

- There are jobs out there that require more education than a high school diploma or GED.
- Required classes are classes you have to take to get the degree you need to get the job you want.

There are also jobs that don't require going to college and pay people less money!

Therefore, if you want to earn more money, go to college!

Another reason to go to college is for personal reasons. These classes teach you things that have nothing to do with getting a job. Personal enrichment classes might include budgeting your money, how to be a good parent, etc.

If you want to go to college, you need to think about the cost. Financial aid pays for classes that will help you get a job or career, but they won't pay for personal enrichment classes.

The very first time I went to college, the Department of Vocational Rehabilitation paid for my college. The next couple of years, my parents paid for it. When I chose to get my social work and advocacy degree, I got a Pell grant because my dad retired, and he was old enough to choose to work part-time. Pell grants, loans, work studies, practicums, and/or scholarships are different ways to pay for college. Scholarships are earned, but financial aid gives you your scholarship.

How to choose what degree you want to get:

- What do you like to do?
- Name as many job options as you can think of that you are good at and that you would enjoy doing.
- Do you want to make any of your hobbies a job?

TO SUPPORT TEAM: If the choice maker will let you, help them choose if college is right for them, and help them find out what they are good at and enjoy so they can find a job that is best for them.

- Why do they want to go to college?
- Does the job they want require going to college and/or getting a degree?
- What are their options for paying for college?

If they want to go to college and they can't afford it, help them work out a way to pay for it. Possible plans could be:

- Part-time job
- Full-time job
- Pell grant
- Work Study
- Scholarship
- Family
- Practicums

Employment

When I was in elementary school, I dreamed of being a schoolteacher for young children around second or third grade. As I got older, my dream job changed.

I remember wanting to go to a different country and preach the Gospel of Jesus Christ. I never left the country. Part of the reason was I needed to take a job skill to the country such as teaching English, giving medical care, etc. I had no skills at that time. I was also dealing with my physical and learning disabilities.

I also remember wanting to be a lawyer to help people with disabilities. I finally realized that being a lawyer would be unhealthy for me. The reason I feel this way is when my stress level is high, I get anxious and panicky. My stomach hurts. I also get sweaty. I have acid reflux and I don't want to feel sick! I refuse to work a job that will cause my disabilities to be worse on a daily basis.

I need a job that will keep me healthy!

I have done volunteer work at the nursing home where my grandfather was living. I decided I would never work in a nursing home! The only way I would volunteer in a nursing home again is if my mom or dad had to live in one, and I'd volunteer there as long as they lived there.

I have had the Department of Vocational Rehabilitation (DVR) place me in sheltered employment three times, but most sheltered employment jobs require using both hands and individual fingers skills. I only have use of my fingers on my right hand, but I have no use on my left hand! DVR placed me there to assess my job readiness skills to figure out what I was good at. I always went prepared for a telephone job. Phone jobs require answering the phone, stuffing envelopes, typing, greeting people, etc. My only problem with this kind of job was that every time they got new software on the computer, I'd have to learn another computer program again and again!

The last time DVR worked with me I got a minimum wage telephone job as a market researcher. I had this job for 1½ years.

I currently want to be a teacher and an advocate for people with intellectual disabilities, but I'd advocate for people with other disabilities too. (At this time, I volunteer.) To me, how a person with any kind of disability thinks is equally as important as their health! I want to teach people with disabilities to make educated decisions. I want to teach them how and why certain things will help them be healthy and how and why other things are unhealthy!

People usually find a job that makes them enough money to pay their bills and to have enough money to have some fun in life, and other people like to earn more money to save for retirement and/or to give to a non-profit organization. Most places of worship are also non-profit.

Some jobs pay more in the same business. How? Some employers pay hard-working employees more than other employees, and other employers pay employees more by how long they have been working for a company. The most common way to make more money in the company is to get a promotion. Higher paying positions have more responsibilities! The higher the position, the more responsibilities there are!

The way to get a higher position in a company is to learn the company's language and the language in your field. Company language is language that is used at a specific company. McDonald's might use different words than Burger King. McDonald's sells Big Macs. Burger King sells Whoppers. You can only get a Big Mac at McDonald's, and you can only get a Whopper at Burger King. Each company has its own language.

Another way to get the job you want to do for the rest of your life is to take any job you can find to pay your day-to-day bills and save money for college. When you graduate from college, you can get the job of your dreams!

Don't Be Afraid to Make a Mistake!

Wisdom comes through the experience of making mistakes and having successes and taking responsibility for both! The reason for taking responsibility for **both** your mistakes and your successes: to learn from your mistakes.

Mistakes help you to know what to avoid so you make fewer mistakes and you know what you did right. You'll feel great when you succeed!

Communicate with people at work. Most people know how to do this. If you struggle with communicating with your coworkers or boss, tell your support team!

Do you struggle with the difference between personal and professional relationships? Do you struggle with setting boundaries at work? If yes, tell your support team.

What is the difference between a career and a job? A career is a job you want to do until you retire. A job is a place where you work until you can find another job. For example, I was a market researcher. I did this job until I needed more time to write my books. Another example is the person who wants to be a caregiver until they retire, they chose care giving as a job—a steppingstone toward their career goal. For the person who is a caregiver until they finish college or until they find a higher paying job, care giving is just a way to make money.

My career goal is to teach people with intellectual disabilities to be their own best advocate, how to set boundaries, how to make choices, and how to stick to the choices they make! Being a social worker is a step toward my goal of being a teacher and an advocate for them.

Here's how to choose the career you want: You start by asking yourself two kinds of questions. The first kind of question is, "What are you good at?" Be honest with yourself! Nobody is good at everything!

- Are you good at working with machines? If so, what kinds of machines?

- Are you good at doing physical labor?
- Are you good at office work? (Things like answering phones, typing on a computer and filing.) If so, how many words can you accurately type a minute?
- Are you good at restaurant work such as being a host, waiting tables, dishwashing, or cooking?
- Are you good at working with the public?
- Are you good at working with co-workers?
- Are you good at working by yourself?
- Are you good at fixing computers when they crash?
- Are you good at working with animals?
- Are you good at working with plants?

The **second** kind of questions is, "What do you enjoy doing?"

- Do you enjoy working with machines? If so, what kinds of machines?
- Do you enjoy doing physical labor?
- Do you enjoy office work? (Things like answering phones, typing on a computer and filing.) If so, how many words can you type a minute?
- Do you enjoy doing restaurant work such as hosting, waiting tables, being a dishwasher, or cooking?
- Do you enjoy working with the public?
- Do you enjoy working with your co-workers?
- Do you enjoy working by yourself?
- Do you enjoy fixing computers when they are broken or crash?
- Do you enjoy typing on a computer and getting into different computer programs? If so, how many words do you type a minute?
- Do you enjoy animals?
- Do you enjoy working with plants?

By doing what you are good at and what you enjoy, you will like going to work every day!

Some jobs don't pay very much, but those jobs are enjoyable. For example, a person in a music career or a career in a religious job might be a low paying job. Religious jobs could be working at your place of worship, working in a religious school, etc. The benefit of working in such a place is that everyone shares your spiritual values. Some people just want to make a lot of money and don't care if their job is enjoyable. Their reward is money! Other people like to earn extra money so they can give money to religious, social, or non-profit organizations.

The more you know about yourself, the easier it will be to find the best match of a job or a career that you will be good at, will enjoy, and will be the right amount of hours!

Know yourself: How long are you **able** to work? Before you look for a job, answer the following questions:

- How many hours can you work before you get tired?
- How many hours a day do you want to work?
- Do you need to work part-time?
- Can you work full-time?
- If you can only work part-time, how many hours are you able to work a day?
- If part-time, how many days a week can you work?
- If you are looking for part-time work, can you work morning, afternoon, or evenings, or any shift they want?
- What days of the week are you willing to work?
- Will you work any day of the week the boss asks you to?
- Will you work any shifts the boss asks you to?
- Are you willing to work weekends?
- Do you have a religion that believes it is wrong to work on certain days of the week?
- Will you work on your days off, if asked?
- Can you work rotating shifts?

If you can't do something, when you apply for a job, write it on the application and while you are being interviewed, tell the interviewer right away, not after you are hired. The boss hires people based on *the boss's* needs. If they hire you, they assume you can work *when they need you*.

Gaining More Independence

Once you have a job and can pay all your required bills, you'll know how much money you have for spending and saving. What you do with the rest of your money is your choice.

The kind of services people usually think about buying are going out to eat, getting cable TV, living alone, buying a house instead of renting, buying a vehicle, etc. The types of products people think about buying are new video games, a new TV, a cell phone, etc.

The two things I am going to write more about in the next couple of chapters are cell phones and the challenges of living on your own. The list of questions I ask in the next chapter will help you to choose if you need or want a cell phone. The questions can be used before you buy most products and services. Use these questions to find out the best quality and quantity for the best price!

It is very important to ask questions before giving money to non-profit organizations, religious organizations, political causes, or candidates.

*Have your support team help you write a list of questions!

*Talk to your support team before giving money to any organization! If your support team has never seen or heard of someone or a company or if they disapprove, don't give money to that organization! Find organizations that they have heard of!

Cell Phones

Here are some words and phrases having to do with cell phones, and their meanings:

Anytime minutes is when you pay for a certain amount of minutes on certain days of the week at certain times. For example, you might have a plan that says that Monday through Friday from 8:00 a.m. to 8:00 p.m. you can talk for 2,500 minutes for $95.00 plus tax. If you go over 2,500 minutes during your billing cycle, you'll pay $0.40 per minute until the next billing cycle starts!

Billing cycle means one month of phone service. The billing cycle could start on the 15th and end on the 14th of the next month.

A monthly plan is a plan you choose that meets your personal needs and wants. Plans could include a family plan with two or more phones, or a plan might be using 3,000 minutes during business hours and have unlimited minutes when businesses are closed. There are many monthly plans to choose from.

Contract is a legal agreement between you and a company. The agreement is written on a piece of paper that is signed by everyone involved. In this case, it would be the cell phone company and the customer. Both the company and the customer have protected rights and responsibilities! If the company breaks the rules of the contract, you are protected. If you break the rules of the contract, the company is protected.

Dropped calls means when your phone hangs up *before* you finish the call.

International calls mean making or receiving calls from one country to another country.

National calls mean making and/or receiving calls from one state to another state.

A computer system is when you make a call and a computer says press 1, press 2, etc. The computer system may make you push many different numbers before you can talk to a real person.

Customer service representative means a live person who helps customers on the phone or in person.

Kickback is when a company gives a customer credit for referring someone to their business and that the new customer starts using their company.

Give a credit means the business will reduce your bill for one month of service, reduce the cost of a product, or a business might give a credit by giving you a gift certificate to use at their store. Each company has its own policies regarding kickbacks and giving credits.

Text messaging means writing a message and sending it from one phone to another phone.

Insurance means protection. If you buy insurance and your phone gets stolen or broken, the company will fix or replace the cell phone for free!

This is my story of when I got my first cell phone and why. I was 28 years old at the time. I got into a verbal disagreement with my boyfriend. When we both calmed down, he told me how to get home *safely* on the city bus!

The bus driver disagreed with my boyfriend regarding the best way for me to get home. The bus driver argued and scared me. It was night, the driver was very loud and was a large man, so I chose to do what he said and got off the city bus where he told me to! It was getting cold and dark at 5:30 p.m. The buses ran less often! The sun was going down which made it hard for a bus driver to see me. The first bus passed me and I panicked!

I was looking for anybody who could help me. Finally, I found a lady walking down the street with thick makeup on her face. I asked her, "Are there any open businesses around here?" She pointed to two uniformed policemen. I asked them for help and they didn't help me. The second bus passed me up 30 minutes later. *Finally, I caught the third bus!* When I got home, I called my boyfriend and told him everything.

Later, my boyfriend was offered two cell phones for the

price of one. He decided I needed a cell phone for my safety, since bus drivers and the police didn't help me.

When his contract ended, I didn't want another cell phone. However, my parents insisted on me getting another cell phone for my safety. They used to think I'd use more minutes on the cell phone in one month than they could pay for! Since they wanted me to have a cell phone and I didn't want one, they bought me a new cell phone and paid the bill every month.

Because my parents were going to buy the phone, they wanted to choose the cell phone company. However, I got to do most of the research and found the company that offered free long-distance calls for the cheapest price *at that time*! It was fun watching the salesman confuse my parents!

Before my cell phone contract was over, another phone company offered me a cell phone. I accepted it. Because I was still under the other cell phone contract with the other company, I was paying two cell phones bills until one contract ended.

The new company charged me around $600. My parents had to keep paying for my old cell phone bill until the contract ended three months later.

I hated my new cell phone because it didn't work at the college. The college was one of its dead spots.

The other problem I had was my mistake! I got into two different cell phone contracts. I should have told the second company that I already had a cell phone!

To correct these problems, I called my State Legislator and made a complaint to the Utility Commission to protect myself. They helped me with my home telephone; however, there was nothing they could do to help me get rid of the new cell phone contract!

Until my older cell phone contract ended, my fiancé and I traded cell phones since the new cell phone didn't work at the college. My fiancé is the same man who had put me on his cell phone plan when the police didn't help me!

Don't loan your cell phone to strangers! If you do, be extremely careful of who you let borrow your phone!

Correcting money mistakes is called being responsible, even if you ask for help. These are the questions to ask when a mistake is made:

- What is the mistake?
- How did I make the mistake?
- How do I correct the mistake?
- How do I avoid making the same mistake?

All these questions help you make smarter choices.

I am glad I made the mistake with a small amount of money before I got married and had children. If I had made the mistake after I was married and had children, it would have been much harder to correct. Also, my husband and children would have suffered financially.

My lesson was that when signing paperwork, I need someone with me!

RESEARCH EVERYTHING!

I made a list of my needs and wants before I started shopping for a new cell phone and company. I also learned to never have two contracts for the same product or service! You can ask your questions online, on the phone, or in the store!

I hate doing financial business online! I choose to do all my research by phone or in person and buy products and services in person!

Here is my partial list of needs and wants to possibly ask all the cell phone companies. I'll show part of my list, so you can think through your needs and some wants regarding cell phones. I need a cell phone company that will:

- Let me talk to a live customer service representative on the phone or someone in the store if I need to.
- I need a customer service representative that understands me and the problem I'm having at the time.
- I need a customer service representative that will take the time and have patience to work with me on the phone or in the store.

- I need free national long distance in all 50 states.
- I need a company that can accommodate my family and my disabilities in the form of assistive or adaptive technology.

After finding out all the cell phone companies that offer adaptive technology devices:

- I would look into the prices for adaptive technology devices. I would want to know if the company provides adaptive technology for free or at a reduced price, or do customers with disabilities have to pay full price?
- In order to receive free or reduced prices, do they need to see proof of disability?
- I need unlimited talk time.

(Use the above process of questions when looking to buy _any_ products and services.)

Most cell phone companies require customers to have a credit card or bank card so the customer can pay a cell phone bill over the phone or the internet.

Businesses accept checks and money orders through the mail. Businesses accept credit cards and bank cards over the telephone computer system.

**The following is research I did on some cell phone companies. There might be new companies out there after this book is in print.

- AT&T 1-800-331-0500 or look in pamphlets www.wireless.att.com
- Cricket 1-800-274-2538 or pamphlets or www.mycricket.com (Note: AT&T has bought Cricket.)
- Verizon 1-800-256-4646 pamphlets or www.verizonwireless.com
- T-Mobile 1-800-937-8997 or pamphlets or www.t-mobile.com

TO CHOICE MAKER: After you find out what you need and want, ask each cell phone company your questions.

It would be smart to talk to your support team about these things:

- What do they believe your needs and wants are regarding a cell phone?
- What's their monthly plan?
- How and why did they chose their monthly plan?
- Why did they choose the cell phone company they chose?
- If you know someone who has never owned a cell phone, find out why.
- If you know someone who used to own a cell phone and doesn't own one now, find out why they got rid of it.

For your financial safety, I strongly encourage you to take someone from your support team with you to the store. Tell them how and when you need their help. You can tell them the questions you want to ask the salesperson.

Considerations for deciding which cell phone company and monthly plan is best for you:

- How important is it to get a live customer service representative?
- How easy is it for you to use the telephone computer system?
- Do you have a computer?
- If you have a computer, do you know how to do business online? If so, do you want to do business online?
- How much time do you have to go to the store?
- Do you need a family plan?
- Do you travel out of town?
- How many minutes do you need?
- How important is mobile-to-mobile minutes to you?

- How much money can you afford for a cell phone?
- How much are you willing to spend every month?
- Are you in the military?
- Are you a student?
- Do you have a disability?
- Are you a senior citizen?
- If you answered yes to any of the last four questions, does the cell phone company give a free or reduced cost when the customer shows proof?
- Does your job provide you with a cell phone?
- Can you use the work cell phone on your personal time?
- Do you think it is important to get insurance on a cell phone?

It would be wise to show your support team the questions you want to ask. If they have any questions for you, answer them honestly, even if you have to look it up and get back to them. If they suggest some questions you should ask the salesperson, ask.

Your support team should be trying *to help you* by asking you questions that help you know what you need and want.

TO SUPPORT TEAM: Let the choice maker know how you made your choice whether or not to have a cell phone. If you have a cell phone, how did you choose your provider? It may also be a good idea to tell them why other people chose different plans and providers.

The main point is to help the choice maker understand how to choose a cell phone provider/company and the monthly plan they need, want, **and can afford**.

Listen with an open mind to the choice maker's answers to your questions. Answer all their questions openly and honestly. Give them information that they don't know and should know. Let them know why some information is important and how to ask those questions!

TO BOTH OF YOU: Talk everything over before you two go to the store. Let the choice maker do the talking until he or she is stuck or asks for help. Then the support person should speak until the choice maker can start talking again. It may also be wise to have both of you call the cell phone stores, go to stores, and shop online together when buying your first and second cell phones.

The Challenges of Living on Your Own

Here are some terms:

Interests: things people enjoy. A hobby is an interest that people put their time, money, and/or energy into.

Goal: something that takes your time, energy, discipline, and willpower to get done. Examples of goals are going to college, losing weight, or saving money for something expensive to buy.

Support group: place you go to help yourself stop an addiction such as smoking, drinking, drugs, or gambling, etc. It could also be a place you go to help you deal with a disability or a family member's disability.

Support network: includes *all* the people that you have around you. For example, your place of worship, needed government supports, your family, and friends. It's important to know who you can call for help when you need it. It is also important to let others know *when you* can be the helper.

After I graduated in 1990, I spent a couple of months living with my parents and I started singing in the choir at church. One of the choir ladies offered me room and board at her house. This was how I moved into the community. This lady and her husband were politically active and that is how I got started in politics.

While I was living there, my parents thought they were taking advantage of me for their political beliefs. I made phone calls for the Republican Action Club. I guess my parents thought I didn't want to do this, and thought these people scared me, or that they were telling me how to vote.

During the 11 months I lived with this family, there were things I did around the house. I was also learning how to ride the city buses and became eligible to ride the disability van. Even though I was involved in ministry and had governmental assistance, something was still missing. Church and these agencies were not meeting my social needs.

When I moved into my own apartment, I had no idea how to

schedule my days and I was bored. Six months after moving out on my own, I had a nervous breakdown and ended up in a mental health hospital for 14 days. Through going to the hospital, I started learning how to plan my days, and I learned how to choose friends and create proper boundaries.

A disability agency helped me realize that because of my physical limitations and my learning disability, I needed someone to come into my home to help me if I was going to live alone. They got an agency to help me with what I was unable to do. The following is a partial list of what this agency can help people with disabilities do. They can help with cooking, cleaning, and personal care task needs! This is a partial list of personal care tasks. They include assistance with bathing, toileting, brushing hair, brushing teeth, help with medication, getting dressed, transferring clients in and out of bed and wheelchair, etc. If this is something you need, talk to your support team.

I started going to the Evergreen Club. The Evergreen Club is a place where people who have mental health issues go. At the time I went there, it was a day program that helped people maintain their social life and helped members with mental health issues get jobs. My reason for going to the Evergreen Club was for social and emotional support while learning how to plan my days!

At that time, I wanted to take care of my grandfather who had Alzheimer's disease so he would be taken care of by family. Other family members chose to put him in a nursing home and I chose to spend my time visiting him in the nursing home until he died.

The members at the Evergreen Club quickly found out that I had a healthy spiritual background and that I knew how to work with the political system. They found out that I talked to the elected officials. The people with mental health disabilities came up to me and asked some of the same things that people with intellectual disabilities asked me, but they'd also say things like, "I do not want to go into the hospital," "I do not want to live in a group home," or "I want to live in a group home or hospital."

I was young and had very strong values. My values included honesty, responsibility, and communication.

The members were coming to me for help instead of going to the professionals. I kind of became a political and religious caseworker in a way.

Politically, I gave them the information they asked for. Religiously, I would only give them information if they let me share my faith with them. I wanted them to understand and apply their faith to their own life.

*I got frustrated and burned out from the Mental Health system after three years at the Evergreen Club because my caseworker would not help me while all the professionals were shoving help down the throats of people who didn't want help.

In fact, I was very, very tired because the people were coming to me for my political knowledge but would not follow through with what I told them. At that time in my life (1993), I didn't understand why the professionals kept those members on their caseload when they refused to accept or cooperate with the professionals. In 1993, if it were me, I'd walk away from someone who let me know they didn't want my help. To me, the professionals were wasting their time and the taxpayer's money, and here I was a willing member who would accept and cooperate with any professional help they would give me. They didn't help me!

It didn't bother me to give my peers political advice along with sharing my faith with them. What I hated was when someone wasted my time. I could have spent that time doing something I wanted to do or helped someone who would accept my help by trying to do what I told them to.

I also started going to college full time in 1993 and I made friends with a person who was violently mentally ill. He didn't drink alcohol or use illegal drugs. I also volunteered my time at a Christian homeless shelter.

TO CHOICE MAKER: Even with my boundaries, I still made a bad choice in choosing a friend. This shows you how setting boundaries will help you make fewer bad choices!

Back to my life story. I chose to be this person's friend for a couple of reasons. I was bored, and this person didn't smoke, drink alcohol or use illegal drugs. Because it wasn't caused by bad habits and he had no control over his temper, I treated it like a disability. I didn't realize his anger was just as dangerous as the person who does drink and use illegal drugs.

As you can see, even though this was a bad choice of a friend, ***I got to learn from my mistake!*** I also remember the good things he taught me and learned from them. Just because he was a bad choice for a friend does not mean he's stupid. In fact, he was very smart!

On one hand, if people would have let me make my own choices when I was growing up, I probably would have had an easier time listening to what my other friends said about him. Since I refused to listen, this is one area I got to learn from my mistake!

In his defense, he never hit me and he never touched me in a bad way! He never lived with me and he never even asked to live with me, probably because he knew if he did ask, I would yell, "NO" and never speak to him again.

The trouble started when I wanted to watch a TV program or do my homework and he wanted my attention. He was bored and he wanted me all to himself, even though I had things to do. I had set up some boundaries for my college schedule, my homework, and most importantly, me!

Remember I wrote about my birthmark on the right side of my face? Well, I guess people in the community, including the law enforcement were asking him, "Did you hit her?" Nobody ever asked me! I thought his behavior was getting crazier because he was getting accused of beating me up. I thought I had to do something so he would calm down, but I didn't know who to talk to so that the law enforcement would know it's a birthmark and *not a bruise*!

I remember hearing about a surgery that could remove birthmarks. October 1993, I decided that I would go through seven of these surgeries. My thinking was, 'If I remove my birthmark, he will be nicer because people will stop accusing him of hitting me.'

The next year was my second year at the Evergreen Club. One friend, who had been in denial of her mental health issue for 20 years, kept getting help she rejected. She would not cooperate with the professionals. At this time, I was not getting the help I needed!

I went back to being politically active with the Republicans until I felt safe in the disability community again.

Just because people are entitled to something does not mean the entitlement should be shoved down their throat. The client should be allowed to accept or reject every entitlement that is offered to them unless rejecting help endangers other people.

I have compassion for people who smoke, drink alcohol or do illegal drugs, but I still have my personal boundaries. I might choose to be around someone who has bad habits, but that's my choice! I support anyone who wants to stop bad habits! However, no one should be forced to stop, but encouraged!

For three years, I watched people go in and out of a mental health hospital. Some people liked getting help and others hated it.

I saw clients stay in denial of their disability, and I watched the system continue to try to help people who *never* realized that they needed help. It was like watching someone addicted to drugs who keeps denying that they have a problem. To me, it might be worth the money to help people who can't see their need for help for five years, but if they still can't see their need for professional help, they should have their case closed until the client seeks professional help!

Help the people who have a mental health issue, who take their medicines as prescribed by the doctor, and do all the right things and **still need** help. If someone admits to having a mental health issue and is smart enough *to know* when to ask for help, there should be money available to help those people when the symptoms show up. It is flat wrong not to!

Help the people who need it, want it, and who put the public in danger because of their disability! If they were a danger to the public and were refusing help, they must get the help or go to jail or prison if they break the law like any other person without disabilities! If there is any money left, help the people who need it, but can't see their need, and will accept help. Don't help people who need and reject help if they are not dangerous!

In 1994, I started attending a weekly Bible Study with people who are physically challenged. Most of these new friends were unable to walk, talk, or use their hands; however, they were very happy people! This was two hours, one night a week, and I really enjoyed myself! These people had no questions or demands! It was a place I could relax to regain my energy and sanity!

Soon after I started that Bible Study, I had to get a no contact order against the angry man. A no contact order is a legal piece of paper a person gets from the courthouse so that the police know that one person is having problems with another person whose name is written on the paper. *In order to get any kind of protection order, one person has to have threatened another person's safety.* Both the victim and the person causing the problem have their names on the protection order.

There are other legal names that these legal papers are called. If you need one, the courthouse can help you figure out which kind of legal paper you need.

The police will never know that one specific person is threatening another person unless there are legal papers showing there's a problem. Without legal papers, the police will never know that there's a problem. *Unless a person's life is in danger at the time they call*, an officer can't help you. That's why legal papers are so very important!

I wanted this person to stay away from me!

As I was continuing my surgeries, I started talking to a lot of volunteers on the phone that worked for a disability agency. The phone felt safe because that dangerous person kept breaking the law by trying to contact me even with a protection order against him.

One volunteer encouraged me to get a music degree since I already loved to sing and sang in the choir. I wanted to be a voice teacher. To become a voice teacher, I would have to go to a lot of concerts that most people dislike. The concerts were instrumental and the singing was in a different language. I did not know anyone who would want to go to the concerts with me, so my dad wanted me to ask the volunteer who encouraged me to get a music degree. My dad was too tired to go out at night because he worked full time and he didn't like this kind of music.

In 1995, I stopped the surgeries, I chose to set a goal and respect my dad's wishes. I asked this person if we could be friends outside work where I was the client and he was the professional. He had no choice! He had to say no and that made me mad! So, I set a new goal! I chose to fight to change that rule! People should be allowed to choose their friends no matter what their job is. People are people and should be able to be friends with anyone they want including clients and employees. There are good and bad people everywhere, including religious people! There are good and bad people in every job. To protect clients, students, residents, etc. this way made no sense to me.

I asked him if he would personally want to be my friend if the rule wasn't there. He said, "Yes, if the rules would let me." That's the reason I felt it was worth fighting for.

The thing that mattered to me was, it should be everyone's choice to say yes or no when they are asked! My dad was supporting me by giving me the money to make the long-distance phone calls to professional organizations and he gave me moral support!

After 1½ years, I stopped trying.

In 1995, I also had to get a second no contact order and chose to continue school. When I realized I couldn't play an instrument and sing at the same time, I quit college again!

This was my last year at the Evergreen Club because the professionals refused to enforce any rules when members were getting harassed by other members. When they were crossing my personal boundaries, there were no consequences for their inappropriate behaviors and actions when their illness caused them to be sick. So, I left the Evergreen for good in 1995.

In 1996, I became more socially involved with my Bible Study friends. Even with their severe disabilities, I enjoyed their friendship because of their happiness!

I had another goal: to get a lady elected to office. I volunteered by calling registered voters! After I tried to get this person elected to office, I got a job for 1½ years as a market researcher.

As you can see, hobbies, interests, goals, and support networks can change over time!

TO CHOICE MAKER: *If* moving out on your own or with roommates of *your* choice is your goal, here's a safe way to do it:

- Know yourself!
- Know your likes and dislikes!

If you don't know yourself very well, you might do things you like, dislike, and/or even hate.

Once you know your likes and dislikes:

- Communicate them!

You can speak, write, draw, or use a combination of ways to communicate, or any other form of communication the other person understands!

If you are unable to communicate clearly with professionals and strangers, your support team might worry about you because when something is very important, you'll be unable to express your needs and wants, and you might be ignored!

- Make your home safe!

Set boundaries! Your boundaries show other people who you are by what you stand for! Set boundaries to protect your:

- Body. One example of protecting your body is telling someone, "Don't hit me!" Another example is, "Don't call me before 7:00 a.m. or after 9:00 p.m.; I need to get some sleep."

- Feelings and Emotions. This is an example of how to set a boundary if someone is hurting your feelings, "If you call me names, I will _____! Whatever you put in the blank, you must do that every time someone calls you that name because when you do the same thing every time, people will know you are serious! If you change your response every time they call you names, they might keep calling you names.

- Mind. This is what I mean by protecting my mind: If someone is asking me for help, I will think of every possible solution to help them. I'll do this a couple of times. If they never take the information, I won't help them in the future. If the person takes some of the information I've given them, I will help them again if and when I have time!

- Time. An example of setting a time boundary is when someone calls on the phone and you have to say, "I only have ten minutes. My caregiver is coming at 9:30." Another kind of time boundary is when you start a job or college, you might need to tell your friends, "I can't go out tonight. I have to study for my test."

- Money. A boundary might be not giving money to panhandlers.

- Property. There are two meanings that I know of for the word property. The first is the land that a building sits on such as a house. There is also personal property which is anything that someone owns!

    For example, I have the right to tell people *don't* smoke in my house. You have the right to tell people how to treat your property!

However, in order for people to respect your boundaries, you must tell them what your boundaries are. You have no right to get mad at anyone for breaking a boundary if you don't tell them what the boundary is! People are only responsible for what they have been told!

You never have to explain why you set a boundary; however, it is smart to tell some people. Why? Out of respect! For example, when I was single, I let a couple of my male friends hug me. When I got married, I changed that boundary. The men who knew me when I was single deserved to know why I didn't want to be hugged by them anymore. However, there was no reason to tell my new male friends.

I tell different people why I have certain boundaries. There's probably no one other than my husband who knows the reason behind every boundary I have.

The reason I share my reasons behind my boundaries is there are times I'd like to understand why the other person has the boundaries they do. I tell family members when there's a reason they should know. Finally, I tell my professionals such as my doctors, counselor, etc. when I think they need to know.

When people know your boundaries and they break them, you have the responsibility to take action. If you don't, they might continue to violate your boundaries because you didn't give them any consequences.

Your action could be a reminder the first time they break them, and then make them face stronger consequences the next time. Handle it friend by friend and boundary by boundary! For example: my best friend will let me call anytime, day or night, but he doesn't let anyone else call in the middle of the night.

- Plan your days (make time and write things down)!

Your plans need to include things that have to be done throughout the day. The kinds of things you have to plan in a day are your job, college classes, possibly homework, doctor's appointments, necessary errands such as grocery shopping, doing things for the kids, etc.

Write down what you do for fun. This includes going to parties, Bible Study, out on a date, or anything else that's fun.

If you don't write things down that you don't do every day such as go to the doctor or out with a friend, you might make plans for two things at the same time by accident!

Contact People

How do I contact people?

- Telephone
- E-mail
- Text
- Snail mail
- In person

Who do I contact?

- Friends
- Businesses
- Family

You might wonder when you will have time to call, text, or e-mail people. It's called multitasking. Multitasking means doing two or more things at the same time! I personally choose to make personal calls only when I'm on the bus/van because I want to keep my business information private! When waiting for or riding the van, I've scheduled my paratransit rides because I can't always do my homework on a moving vehicle.

You need to schedule time to cook, eat, and have fun. These three things can be done while doing other things. You could skip cooking by going out to eat with friends or family.

*All these things have to be taken into consideration when planning out your 7-day week!

*If you choose to live on your own, you will be 100% responsible for everything!

If you need help, that's fine. There are resources that will help people who live alone or with others! There are agencies that send caregivers out to people's homes who have disabilities, but they can't be there 24 hours a day, seven days a week. If you want more information, call 211.

I will write about these agencies in a later chapter.

Making Friends:

Where? The places you go to the most:

- Place of worship
- Religious organizations
- Political organizations
- Place of employment
- College
- Places of shared goals, interests or hobbies. Examples would be sports, music, cars, etc.

Before I go any further, there are two things you should know:

- Don't try to be friends with everybody.
- If you try, you will have no time for yourself.

You can look for friends who have two or more things in common with you.

I have friends who are Christians, who have disabilities and/or are disability advocates. I have a friend that is one of the leaders of the church where I have taught about disabilities and accommodations. This leader has a relative who has become disabled since I first met him.

You can also look for friends by looking at their personality. For example, some people like others who speak with soft voices. If you are hard of hearing, you need your friends to speak loudly! Other personality traits could be honest/dishonest, bold/shy, etc.

Also, there are people you need to avoid, and others that you should avoid.

Who are people we need to avoid? People who will cause harm. These could be people who always ask for money, those that hit you or hurt your feelings a lot or touch you in ways that you don't like.

- Sexual harm = people who touch you in uncomfortable ways and/or sex offenders.

Parents and society protect children from sex offenders. There are places to find out who the sex offenders are that live in your neighborhood, near your job or near your school.

- People who do things that cause you health problems.

People we should avoid are people who have lifestyle differences such as:

- Nonsmoker vs. a smoker
- Non-drinker/recovering alcoholic vs. a drinker
- Non-drug user/recovering addict vs. a drug user
- Sexually moral vs. sexually immoral

There is nothing wrong with any of these groups being friends with each other, but a large part of this chapter has been about setting boundaries.

As a nonsmoker, my smoking friends are my telephone friends. I can multitask by talking to my smoking friends on the phone while I'm doing something else such as doing puzzles. I can't multitask by visiting my smoking friends at work. I either have to go do the things I need and want to do or go outside and visit around all of the smokers, not just my friend! I have two smokers who are family members who I hang out with a few times a year. I don't have time to build a new friendship. Be honest: If someone asks you to be your friend and you don't want to, give an honest reason or don't give them a reason at all!

Build friendships slowly!

- Get to know someone when other people are around
- Get to know someone one-on-one in public

Places that you can get to know someone one-on-one in public would be:

- Restaurant
- Shopping mall

Any place where you can talk with each other around other people is a good place to get to know someone. If you think the person is safe you can start to give them the following information, but not too quickly! The information is yours:

- Phone number(s)
- E-mail addresses

The order doesn't matter. Don't give them both at the same time!

- Physical address (this should be last)

The reason you want to give your physical address last is to keep yourself safe!

Finally, if you have any problems in setting or keeping boundaries, ask your support team to help you!

TO SUPPORT TEAM: Help the choice maker figure out what their likes and dislikes are. This helps them know themselves better!

If they ask for help, help them set their own boundaries! If they don't ask, don't help, but you should still share your history about *why* (and *how*) you set your boundaries! Examples of this would be telling them about your personal mistakes and personal successes. Tell them about books you have read to get your wisdom.

Respect them by telling them:

- When they want to do something that is harmful or unhealthy to their disability!

For example, if the choice maker will die from foods that they eat, then they ***can't*** learn from this mistake! Another health issue: there are things that can make disabilities worse, like drinking alcohol. My personal opinion when it is health related is to have them talk to their doctor. When it is medicine related, have them talk to their doctor and their pharmacist!

- Respect their boundaries, even if you don't agree with them because they are unsafe! If they ask, tell them how you chose your boundaries.

Allow them to express themselves to you and let them practice telling you their different opinions and boundaries. You can give them different responses so they can practice being *firm* with their boundaries. Practice makes perfect!

TO BOTH OF YOU: There is a resource to help people with disabilities pay their bills if the person never learns to pay their own bills. It is called representative protective payee. If you have trouble with money, having a payee might make it possible to live on your own!

There is also another kind of resource that will send a caregiver over to help you do things like bathing, filing your nails, brushing your hair or teeth, getting in or out of bed, etc. They do the housework that needs to be done that you are unable to do because of your disability or disabilities! The name of the resource is different in every State. If you are interested, ask your case manager about getting a caregiver in your home.

If you are unable to do personal care tasks or housework, you can still live alone!

TO CHOICE MAKER: If you are using resources or services you don't want that you are entitled to, explain this to your support team.

As a person with disabilities, I'm asking you to please take care of your health and go to your doctors.

Boundaries for Dating

It is your choice to be in a dating relationship. If you choose to be in a relationship, you should take the time to find someone you can talk with and that you like to be around! It is better to be alone than to have a relationship that makes you feel bad.

This chapter helps you choose your boundaries in a relationship. Boundaries guide your choice(s) in who you choose to date, marry, live with, or any other legal living arrangement in the State you live in!

In an earlier chapter, you chose your lifestyle and what kind of person you want to be! Let's say you chose to never smoke. In this chapter, the question is, is it okay if your date, roommate, or lover smokes?

When you make a choice about living together, dating or marrying someone there are a lot of things to consider. After reading through this chapter, it would be smart to talk to a few people you respect.

If you are a religious person, talk to the clergy at your place of worship, and other men and women you respect. Talk to men and women in all age groups: older, younger, and the same age as you and to your support team! Why? People of different ages and genders think differently.

Religious people can help you make choices that follow your religious beliefs. It would be smart to get information from a couple of friends from each source. Sources include:

- Place of worship
- Family
- Friends
- Library
- TV
- Radio
- Newspaper
- Internet
- Support team

Each person must choose what their personal boundaries are for dating!

First, name all the places where you can meet new people. This includes the mall, the grocery store, school, and work. It also includes public transportation, places of worship, the bar, your hobby organizations, clubs, support groups, doctor's offices, etc.

Which places do you think are safe, unsafe, or neutral for meeting new friends, possible dates, or a lifetime partner?

If you are having trouble choosing, look at what most people who have your values do and say. Here is another way to see if these places are good, bad, or neutral places. Ask yourself the following questions:

- Are you comfortable with the way most of the people behave in that place?
- Would you do and say what these people are doing or saying when you are with friends outside this place?
- Do most of the people there respect your physical, emotional, spiritual, social, and mental boundaries?
- If they disrespect you, how do they disrespect you?
- Is this an unsafe place to find close friends?

These are the questions to help you choose your boundaries! You need to know why your boundaries are what they are! The only reason for explaining your reasons behind any choice you make is that your support team might feel the need to protect you from being taken advantage of. It's easier to protect someone when they know your likes and dislikes ahead of time!

Once your likes and dislikes are known, it might be important for your support team to know how and why you made the choices that you made so they _know_ when someone else is disrespecting you!

If you can _prove_ that you are making your own choices by explaining your reasons for how you made your choice, or why you need or want it and telling them why you want them, then you should not have to be protected! This includes proving to your support team that no one talked you into doing or saying things you really don't want!

It is important that you make choices based on *your* values, needs and wants, which can include other people's opinions. However, you need to make choices by looking at many sources. For example, you could compare dating service prices!

A dating service is a business that helps people stay safe while being in a relationship. Of course, they charge money— that's how they stay in business.

It is important that you need or want a product or service you are paying for. It is important that what you do, how you behave and act, and what you say follows your values!

For example, it's stupid to say, "I am choosing to be friends with Jane because I like her smile or because she said hello to me on the bus!" Those are some of the reasons that your support team might think you need to be protected! Other than that, no one needs to know your reasons for your choices unless you choose to give a reason. It's smart to tell your support team your reasons, but you don't have to.

Keeping Yourself Safe

You can keep yourself safe by finding the answers to what you want in a person *before* you start meeting someone in private. You might want to know about their job, religion, hobbies, etc. (It depends on the kind of relationship you want.)

Finding out some of the information you want *takes time*! If you ask someone everything you want to know about them the first time you meet them, they will either be scared off or will say whatever they think you want to hear!

For example, let's say someone you know won't date anyone who drinks, and they want to date you. They might lie to you so you will go out on a date. If you were the one that drinks alcohol and knew he/she doesn't date people who drink, would you tell the truth? Maybe.

What do you want to know about new people you meet, especially someone you would consider dating?

- You find what you want to know by listening to them talk and by watching their behaviors and actions over time.
- What does she/he say and do when you are not around?
- What do other people say about this person?
- Finally, how long do you want to know them to make sure they are telling the truth?

This is how I safely get to know people:

1) When I meet people face-to-face, I have to see them a lot in public so I know if they are safe and if we have enough things in common to make it worth my time and energy to be friends with them.
2) I listen to their tone of voice and body language. Body language includes looking them in the eye and watching their feet and hands.
3) How do they treat other people? If they scare me, I'll avoid them.

4) I'd keep talking to them at the place we met.
5) If we both decide we like each other as friends, I'll ask if they want to exchange phone numbers.

The telephone is my choice of communication! Some of you might choose to exchange e-mail addresses. Communicating by e-mail is fine if you know what the person looks like! **Never** give any personal information about yourself over the internet unless you have met them _in person_ before communicating online. I will talk more about the internet later in this chapter!

6) If we both have time, I'll make time to get together so we can continue to get to know each other in person even though we will still talk on the phone most of the time. If we don't have time, we'll be phone friends! Next, if you still trust the person, you can exchange e-mail addresses (or phone numbers).
7) Last, if they have proven that they can be trusted, I might give them my physical address. Personally, unless there is a reason they need it, I usually give people my post office address.

Think about how well and how long you want to know someone before giving out your e-mail, phone number or physical address.

Another thing you need to know is you have the right to say no to anybody who is touching you if you don't want them to! You have the right to tell people: "Don't touch me" or "Stop touching me" or "Slow down, this relationship is moving too fast." Moving too fast means one person in the relationship wants more physical contact or emotional support than the other person feels safe giving at the time. Touch can include anything from touching on the shoulder to being intimate. _You_ have control over your body, mind, and emotions! You have the right to accept or reject any kind of touching! **Make your choices wisely**!

Anybody includes:

- Family members
- Boyfriend/girlfriend
- Strangers
- Spouse/partner
- Teachers
- Drivers
- Employers/job coach/co-workers
- People at your place of worship

If someone touches you after you have told them to stop:

- Get away from them.
- Report/tell any adult that you trust that someone is touching you in a way you don't want!
- Make a police report (suggested, but optional).

If you choose to use the internet for the reason of meeting people face-to-face and being their friend or date, be very, very careful! Anyone can be tricked.

If I choose to meet anyone face-to-face that I first met online, the following would be my personal safety plan. (If you or others you trust have a better safety plan or can add to my list, go ahead. Since I don't use the internet much, I asked for help in looking up my safety. *Please send me your suggestions for meeting online first!*)

1) Never send a picture of yourself when you first start writing online.
2) Write your first name only.
3) I'd need to know everything before I'd choose to talk to them on the phone.
4) If at any time I feel threatened, I'd stop all contact!
5) If the person I was writing to or talking to writes or says _anything inconsistent_ to what they have written or said in the past about themself, I'd question them about it. If it still doesn't make sense, for my safety, I'd stop contact.
6) If I choose to meet them face-to-face, then I'd exchange

pictures so I'd know what the person I'm meeting looks like!

7) If you chose to meet them in person, it would be very smart to meet him/her in public places for the first few months for safety!

8) For the first couple of times you meet in person, it may be a good idea to have a friend or family member to sit somewhere else in that place and watch how this person treats you. If your friend or family member feels comfortable, then it would be okay to continue meeting with them **in public** without others around for safety.

9) There are dating services online which will protect people who search for love on the internet. They charge money, but this type of service is worth the price of protecting your life, health, safety, and money. These types of businesses do a background check on anyone you ask them to. They will give you all necessary information about your prospective date. Why? The reason is to protect your life, money, safety, and health.

If you choose to use a dating service to meet people online, please use a business that will check the person out that you are interested in! Please check all the businesses that do this type of work, so you get your needs met at the best price and that you can afford!

Next, when making a choice about your date or who to spend the rest of your life with, it is important to know ahead of time the kind of people that you would consider spending the rest of your life with and who would be a good friend and who you want to avoid.

Before I go on, it is important to note that I believe that everyone should be treated equally! *No one should be put down because they are different. Everyone is to be treated with respect for who they are.*

However, it's *not* the law to be anybody's friend, date, or significant other. It is good to be picky about who your friends are, but not too picky. It is nice that our friends come from different backgrounds whether they are younger or older, were born in a different country, etc. However, there may be some differences in your personal opinion that are not worth your time or energy to understand. When choosing a date or someone to spend the rest of your life with, **be very picky**! After all, that person is the person you *plan on* spending most of your time with for the rest of your life.

For example, how would *you* feel spending the rest of your life with someone much younger or much older than you? If extreme age difference bothers you, don't date someone who is too much younger or older. If age doesn't matter, then you don't need to ask.

Here are two examples from my life. Most of my friends are my parents' age because I have more in common with their values and morals than I do with people my age and younger. So, I feel the most comfortable with older people. I'm willing to be friends with people my age and younger if they come up to me first and don't move the friendship too fast!

Another example, I have had is being misunderstood by people whose second language is English. The first problem is I don't understand the other person's accent. The second problem is the people I've met whose second language is English don't understand riddles, puns and "word play." Word play means taking words or phrases and making a joke. I joke with words without thinking, especially when I'm stressed out. Since they don't understand word play, I choose not to be their close friend, but I'm polite to them and respect them.

Here's something else to be aware of. The following is a list of words and their definitions:

1) Heterosexual: A person who is heterosexual thinks romantically about and has physical urges towards people of the opposite gender.
2) Homosexual: A person who is homosexual thinks romantically about and has physical urges towards those

of the same gender.

3) <u>Bisexual</u>: A person who is bisexual thinks romantically about and has physical urges towards men and women.

People across the USA have feelings about whether heterosexuality, homosexuality or bisexuality are right or wrong. Some people think it's a personal choice. There are people who think it's no one's business except for the people making the choice. There are also people who believe that everyone has to believe their way and has the right to their own way of thinking!

People's reasons for agreeing or disagreeing with same gender marriages could be for medical, religious, political reasons, etc.

My overall opinion is people should only have sex with one person until one of them dies. Why? To protect people's health! I believe in preventing sexually transmitted diseases.

If you have a strong opinion for or against same gender marriages or any other equal rights, get educated and vote. If you are interested in what the current law is regarding same gender marriages, call, write or e-mail your State capitol! A question you may want to ask is, "How does your State interpret holy union?" Another question you may want to ask is, "How does the State interpret domestic partners?"

If you want to change someone's opinion, it is smart to give some facts and reasons. Tell people where you got your information. However, allow them to have their own opinions.

I will give you an example of expressing your opinion. I think people should have sex inside a **legally** binding lifetime relationship! My main reason is religious and my second is health.

I personally believe divorce is okay where there's child abuse. If there is **no** abuse, everything should be done to save the relationship.

- If your relationship needs help, ask your support team

114

about mediation, individual and couples/marriage counseling, arbitration, and reconciliation before divorce is considered!

- I personally think children need two parents.

    Children and teenagers have a lot of emotional needs and they need things which cost money. Two parents can take care of their needs much better than one can. How? After working all day, the working parent is very tired. When there are two parents, one parent can have some free time to do what they want while the other is spending time with the kids and making dinner. The next night, the other parent can spend time with the kids and makes dinner. They both still have to find 1-on-1 time with each kid, and they need to find time for each other and as a family! They also need time to themselves!

- Medical reasons

I believe in having sex with one person to protect from getting a sexually transmitted disease (STD) or giving it to someone else. There are some STD's that can lead to more serious health problems down the line. You can only get an STD by having sex with someone who has an STD.

Basically, if you care about your health and want to have a family someday, save sex for a lifetime relationship!

Two more things I'd like to say about lifetime relationships:

- The next chapter is also about relationships.
- Never rush into a legally binding commitment. You might regret it later. If he/she can't wait for you to feel comfortable, that should be a warning sign for you to think about saying no and to run away as fast as possible.

Some people choose to live together and never get married. Some choose to live together and if it works out then they will get married, and others choose to live in different homes until they get married.

115

In your opinion:

- What are the positives and negatives of living together?
- What are the positives and negatives of dating?

These are some of the things to consider positive or negative:

- Religious beliefs
- How well do you know the person? For example, how long have you known them? Have you known them long enough to know you'll be safe?
- Do you want or need to prove to your support team that you can live alone before living with another person or getting married?

If they ask you to live alone or with a roommate before living with a boyfriend/girlfriend or getting into a legally binding relationship, I think the two main reasons for them asking this of you is to see what you would do when you are left in the house all by yourself. And second, do you know how to protect yourself? If you have trouble with one or both of these issues, hopefully you and your support team will find someone who can teach you the necessary skills!

- Financial reasons?
- Are you choosing to live with the person?
- Is this a person you want to live with for the rest of your life and/or later marry?

If it's only for financial reasons, why not get one or more roommates?

- Whether you are living alone, with a roommate(s), or living together, *are you staying healthy? Is it a healthy place?*
- Is the place where you are living safe?

Safe has two meanings. The first meaning is regarding how much space there is compared to how many people live there. For example, if there are six roommates, two bedrooms, and one bathroom, there would be too many people in that place. For safety reasons, fewer people have to live there. If these six people still wanted to be roommates, they would have to find a bigger place to live!

The second meaning of safety is regarding how safe the roommate(s) or the person you love is. Are the person/people you want to live with abusive verbally, emotionally, mentally, physically, sexually, financially, or in any other way?

Think through the above questions and answer them honestly!

You are free to break off a relationship but consider telling the other person why you're breaking up **if it is safe to**. You would want someone to tell you *why if they* **broke up with you**. If someone ever breaks up with you, would it hurt your heart **less** if they told you why?

From watching other people break up, I have witnessed that the people who have never had sex with their boyfriend/girlfriend find it easier to break up and they might be able to stay friends. It has been explained to me that the more physical touch there is in a relationship, the harder it is to break up. In my personal opinion, breaking up should be the very last option when a couple is married or in another legally binding relationship unless there's abuse or someone's life is in danger! Talk to your support team if there's a problem in your relationship!

The reason for writing the following story is to show you how to put all the pieces together regarding the above list. There is more to the list and the story in the next one or two chapters. Once you see how all the pieces get put together, it will be easier to set your own boundaries!

As a Christian, single, woman who has disabilities, I would identify who I would be interested in before I would choose where I feel safe meeting the right people. For example, I would choose a man who is polite! He must treat me with respect! He must share my faith, even if he goes to a different church.

I would probably want him to have one or more disabilities, but different disabilities than I have. The reason I want us to have different disabilities is so he is strong where I'm weak and I'm strong where he is weak. If we have the same disabilities, we might have some of the same weaknesses. I think that would make life more difficult!

Even people without disabilities have strengths and weaknesses. An example of a couple without disabilities having strengths and weaknesses is a husband and wife team in my church. He works over 40 hours a week and she is the housewife and mom. He gives money to people when he sees them in need. She gets and pays the bills and buys all the things the children need. Therefore, she knows how much money goes for tithing and the bills. She knows how much money the family needs each month, and what should go into their savings account. She sets aside a little money every paycheck for emergencies just in case something breaks down, and the rest of the money is their spending money. He gave her control over the money so they would always have enough money for their own family! She gives him a certain amount of money every paycheck for him to help the people he believes need help.

Can you imagine if both of them were bad with money? What if they were both spenders and givers? That would be bad!! Their bills would never get paid. They would have been living on the street with all seven of their children a long time ago!

Now that I have established who I would consider dating, I can look at places where I would consider meeting possible dates. The places I would consider looking are churches and religious organizations of my faith, disability advocacy organizations, and religious and disability political groups. Places I would never make new friends at would be bars and casinos. For safety reasons, I would never ever look for a date or a friend online. Places I think are neutral are public transportation, college and work.

In fact, I have a friend I met on the city bus. We were friends for one year before we found out we had been going to the same church, but at different times. We were friends for two years before he could think of dating. He was worth waiting for until he was ready. The wait was worth it! Giving him the time and space he needed to feel comfortable with dating made him feel safer with me.

The last thing about dating is the breaking up process. Either person can break up with the other. If you know yourself and set your boundaries, you have a better chance of choosing someone that you will never have to break up with! If you need to break up, there's a better chance that the two of you can remain friends.

When I see my ex-boyfriends, we talk to each other, but we don't hang out in the same places. We don't go to the same church. Instead of trying to change our opinions on our basic values, we agreed that we made better friends than we did as boyfriend and girlfriend.

A basic belief I have from watching other people is not to have sexual contact outside marriage or any other legally binding lifetime commitment, because if there's a breakup, you'll have more respect for each other during and after dating. The more sexual and/or physical contact a couple has before marriage or legally binding lifetime commitment, the *less* respect they usually have for each other and the harder it is emotionally if they break up.

I know from experience that setting the boundary of saving sex until I get married has helped me respect myself and the other person.

Finally, when I broke up with a boyfriend, I gave them a reason!

Now that I have explained the different kinds of boundaries and the process of choosing boundaries by showing you how I chose them and set my boundaries, I will help you choose and set your own boundaries. I will help you do this by asking you some questions. After you answer the questions, talk to your support team.

TO CHOICE MAKER: Here is a list of questions to help you choose your boundaries:

- Are you interested in dating, living with, marrying, or having a lifetime commitment with someone?
- Are you interested in dating, living with, marrying, or having a lifetime commitment with a man, a woman or both?
- Which living arrangement are you comfortable with? Living apart until there's a lifetime commitment or living together without a legally binding contract?
- What places do you think are safe, unsafe, and neutral to meet new people?
- How slow or fast do you want to get to know someone?
- Would days, weeks, months, or years be long enough to get to know someone?
- How do you want to get to know them? For example, would it be in the place(s) that you already see each other at, other public places or in private?
- How long would you want to know the other person before you give them your phone number?
- How long would you want to know the other person before you give them your e-mail address?
- How long would you want to know him/her before you give him/her your physical address?
- Are you interested in meeting new friends or dates over the internet?
- Do you understand and know your space boundaries?
- Are you able to say "no" firmly?
- When you say no and they ignore you, what will you say and do?

If you don't know, ask your support team what they would do if someone ignored their boundaries. When it happened to them, what did they do?

After you answer all the questions you are able to, it is time to tell your support team. They should be quiet until you finish saying everything you want to say. You should be quiet until they are finished talking. If you don't know the answers to some of their questions, tell them you'll find out the answers and get back to them.

TO SUPPORT TEAM: Only ask questions that you think are important and need answers. If you *don't* need to know, don't ask! Be willing to share your answers for every question you ask if they want to know your answer. Be open to sharing your personal experiences so the choice maker will feel safe giving you their opinions and thoughts, especially if they don't want to answer a question. If they don't know the kind of answer you are looking for, ask it in a different way or give them an example.

TO BOTH OF YOU: If your support team is concerned for you in any way and can explain their reason(s) for waiting until a later time to date or get into a legally binding lifetime contract, trust their advice. If you don't understand, ask someone else on your support team to explain it and then make your choice. Know yourself well enough by setting your boundaries!

Dating and Marriage: Protecting Yourself from Sexual Harassment

The first guy I was interested in was very good looking in my opinion. All the girls liked him! He was a partier. I wanted to party and I wanted to dance. Someone finally told me that the parties I was interested in had smoking, alcohol, illegal drugs, and sex outside of marriage. I was shocked and disappointed! I assumed if they were telling me the truth that these teenagers would be arrested for breaking the law because they were too young to smoke and drink. Drugs were never legal at any age!

The two of us never dated because we were too different, and I am glad because he dropped out of high school when he finished 11th grade and became a teenage alcoholic. The Lord provided my parents to protect me from being emotionally hurt by this relationship.

When I was in the 10th grade, a senior in the school choir, John, wanted to invite me to his youth group. Being sensitive to the fact that I already attended another church, he wrote my parents a note asking for their permission to take me to his youth group. Mom said yes. I went and I liked it, so my parents let me continue to go.

Eventually, I started going to that church on Sunday mornings. This was in October 1987. In March 1988, I accepted Jesus Christ into my heart and became a born again Christian. This began a new spiritual journey for me. **This is when I made the choice about God in my life**! I no longer went to church because I had to. I wanted to!

My parents gave me the freedom to choose between going to John's church and going to their church. They allowed me to be different from them! Being a senior, John wanted me to start a Bible Club in the high school. I laughed and said, "Yeah, right, whatever you say." After that, I didn't think much about it.

Why do I share so much about my faith? Faith helped me make my own choices!

122

People asked me, "How did you get your parents off your back?" and people tell me they want to get married. Therefore, I am sharing how my faith in God helps me do everything that all U.S. citizens should have the right to do!

The summer after I trusted the Lord, I was at a friend's house. I was 17 years old. His dad had this very strange game of guessing people's weight that made me feel very uncomfortable. Since I didn't know why it felt wrong, I played the game, but I tried to put him in as much pain as possible because it felt so wrong! I found out later how bad the game was.

Throughout the day, he was drinking alcohol, but he never offered me a drink. He told my parents that he would drive me home and my parents said, "No." Their reason for saying no was that they could tell that he had had too much to drink and should not drive!

It's been more than 20 years and I have seen him twice since then. The first time was an accident and I was safe because other people were there. The second time, I sought him out by phone only because he is my friend's guardian and I wanted his permission to do something with his son. However, I never did and will **never** give him my physical address because he frightens me!

Since I am respected by people with disabilities for becoming as independent as I wanted to be, including my dating life with some guidelines, I respect the people I have chosen to watch out for me. Therefore, I will continue to be protected. I have a true example below that explains what you just read.

After I chose my boundaries, I chose my own friends. I chose a group of friends and family members to help me choose if my future friends were good, bad or neutral, considering my values.

Neutral in this case means nobody can see that there's anything wrong and dangerous. You'll have to use your judgment. Get to know them slowly and use caution.

Good choice in this case means, knowing that a person has your values or respects your opinions and choices.

In 11th grade, there was a guy who had the same physical disabilities as I have, but his disabilities were more severe than mine. However, he tried to undress me in the basement of the school. I prayed that the Lord would protect me and He did; I was able to get away.

I ran up the stairs and to the special education room and told the teacher. Her response was, "That's not my problem. You need to learn to get along with your peers." He stared at me the rest of the school year. I also told my parents and they acted like it was not a big deal. I begged my parents to let me go to a Christian school.

I had decided I wanted to be a music pastor's wife and a stay-at-home mom. I came to that decision because of my church values, committing my life to Jesus Christ, and growing up in the school choir. Also, in 11th grade, there was a guy at church that I had a crush on, but I was too shy to tell him. We were friends, but we never dated.

He played many instruments, sang beautifully, and planned on going into the music ministry when he graduated high school. He was an encourager. Many times, I have told him I wanted to do something such as wanting to be a lawyer and he told me, "Go for it," in the same encouraging way I encourage anyone who talks to me about being more independent. I'll say to go for it and give some suggestions of how to reach their goal!

When I entered the 12th grade, my parents forced me to go to the *same* high school instead of letting me go to a Christian school. The guy who tried to undress me in the basement of the school *kept* bothering me in my senior year. My parents said I couldn't go to the Christian school for three reasons. The first was transportation, and I didn't drive. The second reason was I would have graduated one year later. Last, I needed the resource room for some subjects. At the time, the school didn't have a resource room!

I also met Mark N. while I was in the 12th grade. He had many talents and the ability to be a cook, a weatherman, and an organist. He loved the Lord with all his heart. I was scared to death of the other guy who had tried to undress me, so I stayed very close to Mark. We made a cute couple. Mark and I walked with opposite limps, so we were constantly walking into each other or away from each other. We were in resource science and choir together the first semester. One day, we were standing in the front of the class and he announced, "You are looking at my future bride." He never asked me if I wanted to marry him. I stood there in silence and shock and nodded yes.

He lived in a foster home and his foster dad thought I was a bad influence on him, so we could no longer see each other, and the foster father told another foster child to report back *if* he saw us talking to each other. I was very upset, but instead of turning to alcohol, drugs, cigarettes, gambling, or another relationship, I was bound and determined to hold onto this relationship until he could speak for himself.

Remembering John's request for me to start a Bible Club, I spent my extra energy fighting for a Bible Club. I got 40-45 students to sign a petition. It would not have taken effect until the next school year, after I graduated, but I felt I would be helping future students have a positive way of coping with life. While Mark N. was a senior, I became very busy. I made a friend named Mark R. who was a preacher's kid. When Mark N. graduated from high school, he never invited me to his graduation. With pressure from the government, he moved into a group home, so I broke off the engagement.

On the rebound, I got engaged to Mark R. On the rebound means getting into another relationship without letting your broken heart heal. My engagement with Mark R. was shorter than it was with Mark N. After I broke up with Mark R., I stopped dating for about two years. Being single was fine with me.

During this time, I became friends with a man who didn't drink, didn't smoke, and didn't use illegal drugs; however, he had an anger disorder as a mental health issue. I thought this was safer than anger caused by alcohol or illegal drugs. I am a gentle person.

About nine months after knowing him, he started trying to

control my life by demanding my time. I would not give him my time every time he demanded it! He bothered me on the phone, and I eventually changed my phone number. He called the phone company and told them that he was my husband and needed my phone number. The phone company called me and told me what had happened. I had to vote under my old address for my safety. I also got a post office box. This was a two-year nightmare.

Finally, I had to move because when he violated my protection order, the Sheriff's department refused to help me because I never lived with him, had no children with him, and I was not in a life or death situation! The mental health agency would not help. They said he had no control over what he did because he had a mental illness.

While waiting to catch a bus, there was a different man who said he used to go to my church. I had seen him on the bus many times in the past. From watching his actions and listening to him talk, I didn't think he ever went to church. One day we were waiting for the bus together and he asked me, "Is it all right if I feel you?" I shouted, "No," and moved to the other side of the bus stop! He respected me. I chose to never speak to him again, but after seven years I'd smile or say, "Hi," in passing, but I still won't talk to him.

In 1995, I went to the Spokane Gospel Jamboree. This was a place where people gathered to sing together two nights a week. The jamboree was a better option than going to a bar. There I met Ron. He was interested in me and he also had disabilities, just like all the other men I've dated. He was a Christian, so I decided to give him a chance. I dated him for two weeks and found out he lied to me twice, so I broke up with him because I'm honest. I hate lying. I can handle different opinions, especially when there's a reasonable conversation! Lying crosses one of my boundaries!

At the Spokane Gospel Jamboree, there was a 19-year-old man, Carroll, who ran the soundboard. He was in the Air Force stationed at Fairchild. His eyes were as soft and gentle as the man who wanted to be a music pastor. This was strange to me because I was judgmental of people in the military because I thought war was wrong! I also hate guns. I hated war so much that I attended a no war protest in 1991.

Dating Carroll was very challenging. He surprised me because I thought that all the people who were in the military and who carried guns were loud and controlling. He was so quiet, gentle, and peaceful. I was always afraid he would be forced to move to another base or worse yet be called out to war. We dated for nine months, broke up for nine months, and got back together for two weeks. Then he got out of the military for medical reasons and I never saw or heard from him again.

Part of the reason I never heard from Carroll again was I changed my phone number and moved. Then something very strange started happening. I started receiving phone calls from Air Force Bases all over the country, but I wasn't afraid. I just thought Carroll was playing mean jokes on me. But how could he? I had a new phone number. My phone number had never been in the phone book. After all, no one from the Army, Navy, Marines, or Coast Guard called me, only people from the Air Force Bases and pilots. So why did they start calling me just after my military boyfriend walked out of my life? It was weird. Every time I received that type of phone call, I would remember Carroll and start crying.

Someone finally explained it to me. I knew Carroll well enough to know that he would never give someone's phone number out unless he had their permission, and I also knew he did not have that much power. I also got four calls from other countries. I also had pilots calling me. They would call me asking for catalogs and wanted to buy different things.

One day, a pilot from California called and said, "I think I got the wrong number." I cheerfully said, "Oh, let me guess, you're looking for Survival Inc." and I gave him the correct number.

He asked me if I got a lot of calls like this and I told him I did. I was so excited that I finally got to ask someone where my number was listed at! He explained that people were finding my phone number in a newly printed survival training handbook.

I said, "That's nice to know. May I have the correct phone number to give to all the other people looking for Survival Inc.?" He gave me the number and I put the correct number on my answering machine. I got to play the part of a telephone operator until I changed my number.

We talked for 3½ hours. We talked about flying, religion, the disabled population and what people with disabilities can do, and politics because it was an election year. When we got done talking, he asked, "Do you mind if I call you again?" I told him he could. Today, he's one of my best friends!

He's a great friend, but I would never marry or live with him! His name is Randy. He came up to visit me and took me flying at the local airport. I got to be a co-pilot, and I absolutely fell in love with flying. I made a choice to never marry a man who was afraid of flying. My parents and Randy also helped me fly to California for my birthday and I got to fly again.

Later that year, I met Eli and became his friend. When I met him, he was very sad because two family members died and a third almost died. Being very sad when someone you love dies is called grieving. I sat down in front of this person in a wheelchair that was with Eli and in a happy voice asked, "What is your name?"

Eli said, "He can't talk."

So, I looked at Eli and asked what his name was.

He said, "Joshua."

I said, "It's nice to meet you. I am Tiffani." I was pointing above Joshua's wheelchair and asked Eli, "What's that thing?" It was a kangaroo feeding tower. I asked, "Can he hear?"

Eli said, "Yes."

Finally, I asked, "Can I talk to him?"

He said, "Sure," with a big smile.

I talked to Joshua for 20 minutes before I said another word to Eli. We talked until we got off the bus together. Later, we found out we lived across the street from each other. I saw them on the bus a couple more times and always sat beside them. I said, "Hi" to both of them by name, and Eli would say, "Who are you?"

I would tell him, "I am Tiffani." About the fifth time, I thought, 'This is crazy. I'm going to find out why Eli never remembers my name when I'm so friendly to them.' So, I asked him and he said, "Because I'm legally blind and I can't recognize people by sight. They need to tell me who they are."

One day, I finally asked Eli, "Don't you ever get a day off?"

Looking confused, he finally said, "I'm not his caregiver. I'm his father."

We eventually started spending our free time together. I found out he loved to fly. In fact, he was studying to become an astronaut before he lost his sight.

I found out that we shared the same faith. We went to the same church. He used to be a music pastor and I have ministered through music in the choir. We both had disabilities and we both had compassion for people with disabilities. He was a caregiver and I wanted to be an advocate for people with intellectual disabilities by standing up for their rights and fighting for them to have the same freedoms people without disabilities have! We both loved music. He was a semi-professional musician, vocalist and guitarist, and I loved to sing.

We also dislike the same things which was very important. Neither one of us wants to live with or kiss a smoker! We talk to our family and friends outside when they are smoking. He will wait for his friends to finish smoking and come inside! We both refuse to drink alcohol! We never hang out with people who drink alcohol to get drunk! (We both have friends who are recovering alcoholics.)

After we knew each other for two years, we decided to start dating. We dated for one year and we felt that God was leading us into marriage! We were engaged for a long time—at least one year before we got married. We knew each other a total of four years before we got married.

*Because of all the things I looked for in a man, I was able to narrow down my choices regarding who I would choose to date to keep myself healthy and safe and hopefully marry.

Eli passed both my parents' and my inspection. He passed my inspection because we have so much in common. The three best things about Eli are his:

- Faith in God
- Honesty
- Open communication

His faith in God shows through his honesty and open communication! We have the same belief in God, and he also believes that honesty and open communication are the best policy!

The more things you have in common with someone, the better the chances are that your relationship will work out. It also takes honesty, open communication, and finding the middle ground. How you handle differences of opinion with other people will help you communicate with anyone.

Eli said, "It was traditional for the bride's parents to pay for their daughter's wedding." The reason I share this is, weddings are usually expensive and parents are generally concerned for their children even when their children are adults. They are even concerned for their adult children who have no disabilities! If her parents approve of her fiancé and it is her first wedding, they will probably pay for as much of the wedding that they can afford! (If her parents can only afford to pay for part of the wedding, the bride should pay for the rest of the wedding!) It would be nice to get the man's parents' approval too. A honeymoon follows a wedding! The groom usually pays for the honeymoon which is very expensive! It's not tradition, but it is possible that if the groom's parents approve of the bride, they might help the groom pay for the honeymoon.

Domestic partners are a new enough concept that there are no traditions that I'm aware of. If you are interested in being a domestic partner, ask someone with more knowledge.

Since Eli and I were both adults with two functioning

households, when we got married, we were given a lot of cash as gifts. We used that cash to pay for our honeymoon.

If your parents find more bad things than good things in most people, find a trusted friend who you think will tell you the things you need to know to make an educated choice about possible friends and things you are interested in. For example, before I made my choice about alcohol, I asked my dad about it because I was going to be 21. I thought it might be wrong, but I didn't know why. My dad responded, "You take medication and I don't!" The tone of voice he used when he answered me was very "offensive" even though the advice was right! (Offensive, in this case, means putting me down.) So, I asked a trusted friend at church. His response was, "If it's not good for a child, then why is it good for an adult?"

I took that answer to heart about everything from smoking, dancing, to sex before marriage and more. Choosing a lifetime partner is a very serious choice, so it would be very smart to explain to your support team why you would want to spend the rest of your life with that special person. Let your whole support team ask all the questions they want to ask and answer them **before** you make **your final choice**!

TO CHOICE MAKER: To protect yourself from sexual harassment, domestic/intimate partner violence and from being stalked, find out what these things are. It would be a good idea to talk to your support team and see if they have any concerns.

Sexual harassment, domestic/intimate partner violence, and stalking *are illegal*!

Tell your support team:

- What *your* boundaries are.
- How you will make others respect your boundaries!

For example, a lot of religious people may say they refuse to have sex before they are married. They may enforce it by going out with their date in public or going on a double date. A double date is when two sets of friends go out together with their own

131

date. For example, Heidi wanted to go on a date with Sam, but she doesn't know him very well, so she asked April if April and Steve would go on a date with them. That's a double date!

Ask yourself about both of your personalities:

- Are you soft spoken? Are they?
- Do you like to fight? Do they?
- Do you like to share in making choices? Do they?
- Do you like to talk through problems? Do they?
- Do you like to be calm? Do they?

For example, I make the choices about things inside the house. Eli makes the choices about the outside of the house. There are two things we consider when making choices about the inside or outside. Can we afford it? Can I, as a person with a physical disability, also use it? An example is we have a large screen TV because Eli is legally blind. If we both had good vision, we could have a smaller TV.

TO SUPPORT TEAM: Accept that the choice maker will have different opinions than you. They will want to date different people than you might want them to. However, if you stop the dating process, they will never be able to know who they like and who they'd refuse to date. They won't know why they feel/think that way!

I'll never know why I dated a man in the military when I am terrified of guns. However, Carroll had a soft voice, and I assumed all people in the military were mean. Only in my worst nightmare would I have ever considered dating someone in the military or a police officer. As of my wedding date, I will *never* date because I am married.

These are the things protected people should do when learning how to keep themselves safe: They should explain their reasoning *when learning to* make healthy and safe choices! It would be smart to always explain to yourself (and possibly your support team) how and why you choose the friends you've chosen!

**The motive for wanting to know the choice maker's choices and reasons is to find out which choices have been made by them and which choices they were talked into.

The support team should only have the protected person explain themselves when they believe it is necessary, so the choice maker doesn't feel like they're in a courtroom.

If you want them to share their opinion and they don't want to, share how you made your choice(s) on the same subject!

Children

When I was growing up, I wanted a traditional family. Traditional family means the husband works outside the house while the wife stays home doing the housework and raising the kids. I also believed in being active in the community.

In my late 20's, I thought having children was a bad idea for me!

When I went to school to get a job working with children aged from birth through six years, one of my teachers was very discouraging! They knew I had disabilities and thought the accommodations I asked for were unreasonable!

My school counselor told me parenting my children would be different than taking care of children professionally. The reason I was having trouble was because of my physical disabilities. I had no fine motor skills for changing diapers.

With my learning disability, I had problems with change! Change in this context means as the children grow older, the rules change. As children get older, the rules of what they physically can do and are allowed to do will change.

People who have mental health issues and intellectual disabilities have told me very bad true stories about Child Protective Services (CPS) getting involved in their lives before or when their child was born. I finally saw it for myself and I was told about the CPS process in one of my classes.

It would be smart if social service agencies would start teaching expecting moms and dads how to be healthy and safe parents when the mom is pregnant.

A responsible person would ask for counseling or parenting classes before the mom gets pregnant or delivers.

From what I have seen, CPS takes children away from parents who have disabilities. They rarely give their children back even when the parents can show that they have learned the skills to be healthy and safe!

When I got married, I married into a family with many

children, mostly adults. They were all my husband's children. This makes me a stepmom. One adult son was still living at home and being taken care of because of his intellectual disability. My husband also adopted his grandson. When we got married, we were raising our adult son and grandson.

At first, my husband was the stay-at-home parent while I was going to school or visiting my friends with intellectual disabilities. Then Joshua, our son, went to be with Jesus, and my husband was without a job for five months.

In the next few paragraphs, I am going to state my personal observations from watching people, and the things I personally learned in a class titled, Understanding Child Abuse. I am going to talk about the different kinds of parenting.

One popular kind of parenting that society looks down on is *single parenting*. The reason society looks down on single parenting is, they usually don't have enough money to raise kids! I have watched single parent and two parent families and have noticed single parents have less patience because they are more tired than two parent families! The reason for this is, one parent is doing *all* the housework and earning *all* the money for the household. They are more tired than two people who are sharing the childcare, working outside the home, and housework, etc. I am aware of a few women who felt cheated because they got pregnant when they were too young.

Another reason society might look down on single parent families is when a married couple needs a little government help, a lot of times the government can't or won't help the two-parent family or tells them they are eligible for something they already have and don't need.

For example, I have seen a married couple who had four children apply for medical assistance and be denied, but they were eligible for food stamps. Their rent, electricity and phone bills had been paid and they had enough food in the house. However, single parent families are eligible for everything they apply for, making them totally dependent on the government and upsetting taxpayers!

Married couple parenting is a kind of two-parent family that is very common. Money-wise it is the best kind of family because some jobs will give the spouse and the children medical benefits. Churchgoers seem to view being married first and having children second as "the right way." From people I talked to who have had children outside marriage, most of them have said if they could do it again, they would get married before having children. Most of the people I talked to were churchgoers. Some said they would have had fewer children. Other people thought they would save more money or start buying a house before having kids, and others would choose to never have kids.

Blended families are when both spouses bring their own children into a marriage. The newest parent to the child and the newest child to the adult is the step side of the family meaning the stepparent/stepchild. The parent that is originally attached to the child is the natural parent.

When my husband and I got married, he brought four children and I brought no children into our marriage.

Blended families are probably the most common two-parent families because the divorce rate is so high! Since this group of two-parent families are also married, they get the same medical benefits that first time married couples get.

Due to the special problems blended families have, some churches have a ministry geared for blended families. They may have ministries geared for different ages of children; elementary, middle school, and high school kids who are stepchildren. Some churches have a ministry for stepparents.

Then there are churchgoers who judge them. I will never let a judgmental person bother me whether they are a family member, someone who works in a social service agency, or are a friend. If it's important to me, then I make them explain why they are judging me. My faith in Jesus Christ is my primary way of keeping my self-respect along with ignoring the comments of judgmental people.

The natural parent is the adult responsible for their children and must make sure that every adult who lives in their house is safe for their children to be around.

In my personal opinion, living together sets a bad example for children communication-wise because when adults walk away from a commitment anytime there is a disagreement instead of working things out, the children learn to avoid confrontation. People should learn to work through arguments and disagreements before becoming parents. It's also smart to commit to never divorce over arguments and disagreements!

Here is an example of proper confrontation: Let's say a cashier at the store kept more money than they should have for something you bought. When you notice this, it is proper to go back to the cashier *with the receipt* and get the correct amount of money back. It would be wrong to say, "Oh well," and walk away!! **No one has the right to take money that doesn't belong to the business!**

The worst part about living together in my opinion is, most people who live together only do so to pay the bills. Even if that's your reason and you are not looking for a relationship, anyone you live with still needs to be a safe person!

If you are going to live together or have a roommate(s), you *need to choose carefully* if you want to have child(ren) in the future. You need to make healthy and safe choices if you want to keep your kids.

Relatives and your support team need to know that your children are safe with any adult that's living in your house.

Your living arrangement is a choice, but be careful when a child is in your home because CPS has the responsibility and the right to come in and take your child(ren) away if they think the children are in any kind of danger!!

Foster parents are parents who take children into their home *temporarily*! Foster children might live in many foster homes before they are adopted.

Foster children could have any of the following problems. They may have been:

- Neglected
- Abandoned
- Abused

There are many types of abuse:

- Emotional
- Mental
- Verbal
- Physical
- Sexual
- Social
- Spiritual

Children might be in the foster care system for many different reasons. Possible reasons:

- Their parents died.
- Their parents broke the law.
- Their parents use drugs and alcohol.
- Their parents couldn't afford to take care of them.
- The State won't allow parents who have disabilities to raise their children *unless they can prove they can*!
- The parents can't deal with their child's disabilities.

There may be other reasons I can't think of.

Children may come into the foster care program with the following issues:

- Behavioral problems
- Mental health issues/mental illnesses
- Parents or children with drug and/or alcohol problems
- Parents or children who have intellectual and/or physical disabilities
- Children who are in trouble with the law

Talk to your support team if you want information about the foster care program in your state!

Every State has their own foster care laws. Some States may pay a person to be a foster parent. How much? I don't know. It depends on how hard a child is to take care of, how much damage a child does to property, or the age of the child. Call or e-mail the social service agency that takes care of the foster care program in your State. You can look up the laws for foster care in your State.

Foster parents *must be* strong emotionally to handle the State bringing a child in and pulling a child out, sometimes without warning and with no time to say goodbye. That's hard!

I am only aware of one case where a foster parent called the State and told them to get the child out of their home because the foster child kicked and bruised another child. The child who was kicked was 100% unable to protect himself. This was very unsafe! All children must *be safe at all times*! You must protect your natural children and foster children equally! If it's impossible to keep your natural children safe, stop being a foster parent until it's *safe for everyone*! Let the State take care of the foster children.

Some foster children might damage property or break the law. What would you do if or when foster children did something wrong? Be careful and creative! From things I learned in an *Understanding Child Abuse* class, I will never be a foster parent. I don't have enough energy and I don't have the emotional strength to cope with the State popping in and taking a child or dropping a child off **unannounced** or in the middle of the night.

Adoption is legally giving child(ren) a new set of parents. The legal process of adoption is different in every State! The legal process is different in every country of the world. There are family adoptions where grandparents have adopted their grandchildren. Other family members can apply to be adoptive parents only when the State says that both natural parents are *unable* to raise their kids.

Strangers can also adopt children! However, whether it is a family or stranger adoption, the State has to be the one to choose the adoptive parents!

If you are interested in adopting a child or teenager from another country, there is a whole different process.

The government *must be* involved to check out how safe the family and the house is so they know the kid(s) will be living with safe people and in a safe home.

If you are interested in adopting a child, contact your State Social Services agency.

My personal experience with family adoption was the birth parent making our life a nightmare. My husband adopted his grandson. Life was hard on my husband because there were times the grandson or I asked him to do something that he legally could not or would not do. Most of the time, it was the birth mother who wanted something. He had to make the hard choices for his grandson's health and safety. She was angry that I could legally make choices for her child.

TO CHOICE MAKER: Before I go any further, I want to make something clear about a two-parent family. Even though I write about two-parent families in a very positive way, *if* there is *ever* any danger to any child(ren), talk to your support team to make plans together for *everyone's* safety and health!

There *might not be time* to work out a plan together if there's ever a health or safety emergency!! If you don't communicate before a crisis, you will have no say in what happens! No one ever plans on having an emergency!

If there is a crisis, when the crisis is over, there will be time to talk it out. Find out what every person's ideas are for keeping children and the person with a disability safe, now and in the future. (Children's safety must come before the adult's safety.)

- If the person with a disability has a medical crisis that is temporary, where does the parent want his or her children placed until the parents are able to get their kids back?

140

- Where would the parent want their children placed if the parent is unable to regain taking care of the kids?

Other kinds of temporary emergencies could be being stranded or stuck in another city or State because of grounded airplanes due to the weather.

If parents are out driving and are in a car accident, what's the backup plan?

The types of things parents would want in a plan:

- Who should the babysitter call if the parents are late and are not answering their phone?
- How long should the babysitter wait before they start to be concerned? (Just in case there is a traffic jam, should the babysitter wait an extra half hour before they start to be concerned?)
- Is there anything the children will need (i.e., medication) if the parents are running late?
- How can the babysitter calm the children down if the parents are running late?

There should also be things in place to protect the parents:

- A medical alert necklace or bracelet
- Have a medical advance directive
- Have a mental health advance directive (if appropriate)!

TO BOTH OF YOU: Listen to your protected person even if you disagree.

If your relationship is unsafe and you have children, there's counseling for the victim (the person who is getting hurt). There is also counseling for the person who is the accuser if the accuser will accept help! There are different ways to get away and to stay away from someone for a short time or forever. The person who is being hurt needs to learn new boundaries and why new boundaries are needed while the support team stays temporarily

141

in control! The support team *needs* to stay in control *until* the new boundaries have been set and kept consistently!

Consistently means giving the same reason every time to the same person if you never want to see them again! For example, if he or she asks you if you want to go out on a date and this person has hit you, your answer should always be no! Your reason(s) for saying no should always be the same! If your reason for saying no is different every time, you might answer yes when you want or should say, "No."

However, if there is a person that you want to go out with, but you can't at the time, let them know that you want to but can't right now. You might also tell them when is a good time.

There are ways that the police recognize when two people are supposed to stay away from each other. It is still legal and within the law. However, if you avoid going through the court, you are showing that you might want to get back together with them in the future. DV means domestic violence. Accused person means the person who is being accused of doing a crime, but not convicted of a crime.

Separation means getting away from each other for a short amount of time and possibly getting back together in the future. The set time is agreed to by both people in the relationship. Mediation is finding a neutral person who will help everybody come up with a workable plan for them and keep it out of the court system. Arbitration means all people involved have to go a step above mediation and have someone else put an agreement on paper that is a legally binding contract. There is also marriage and couples counseling. IF both people will accept their share of the good things and the bad things, marriage and couples counseling works. It doesn't work if one person is blaming the other person for everything that has gone wrong and is going wrong in their relationship.

If an accused person is being accused or convicted of domestic violence, **perpetrator's treatment might be available!

*Parenting plans, supervised visits, paying child support, etc. are some ways an accused or convicted parent might be able to work his or her way back to being trusted again.

My husband taught me that our children's needs come before the parents' needs. Needs include:

- Shelter (housing)
- Electricity
- Clothing
- Food
- Quality time every day with every child
- Phone
- Childcare
- Have a plan when a child gets sick at school

It is necessary to have a phone so the doctors, your child's school, etc. can be called in case of an emergency! Parents' needs come second!

Childcare is necessary until the children are old enough to be alone.

When it comes to everyone's wants, if there is enough money in the budget, it would be nice to consider every family member's wants. There is no rule that says one person's wants comes before another person's wants. When there's not enough money for everyone to have what they want, every family still has its own way of choosing if and when the wants get met.

When a child enters school, music and sports may become important in the child's life. Extra activities cost more. Some families might be eligible for scholarships. However, music and sports are wants, not needs! If there are grants or other ways to pay for all the music and sports your children are interested in at school, look into them.

My child goes to a private school and the parents have to pay for afterschool sports. Since sports are a want, he must keep his grades up and be more responsible in other areas. We will pay for his sports and do our responsibilities to make him successful in sports if he does what he is supposed to! That includes asking for help when he needs it. These rules apply to music also!

Before you make a choice to be a parent, it would be a wise idea to read up or have a friend help you look up information on every kind of parent you are interested in becoming (adoptive, etc.). Also, it would be wise to talk to the kind of parents you are interested in becoming, like natural, blended, etc. This kind of research helps everybody make choices. You can gather information from the news, the library, relatives, radio, friends, your advocates, your doctors, the internet, and your support team.

Ask your support team what they see as *your* strengths and weaknesses. (I would choose friends and family from different walks of life, like someone from church, friends who have the same disabilities, my best friend, and my mom.)

From what I have seen, the people who only get practical advice are very discouraging! The people who talk to spiritual people are given so much positive information that they are more prepared to be a parent. Spiritual people know how to say what is positive and good, such as they're honest, etc. However, what does honesty have to do with the ability to change diapers or cook?

The people who are giving spiritual and practical information are wonderful. Sometimes spiritual people or people without religion can give you both spiritual and practical information.

I have spiritual friends who helped me raise my children with the values I want them to have. They encouraged me. Practical people have taught me things I need to know to keep my children safe!

Your practical friends can help you by taking an honest look at your ability to take care of children or your ability to learn. If your trusted people have concerns, find out what their concerns are.

You and your four friends or family members need to be free to point out your strengths and weaknesses. It needs to be done in a way society calls constructive criticism. Constructive criticism means saying things in a way that will help someone do something better without putting them down. For example, by taking parenting classes, it may help you to know what to expect from a child. The only requirement for the parents is: Both parents *must attend all* the parenting classes! These classes can provide needed accommodations to parents who have disabilities to make their home healthy and safe. The accommodations may be education and knowledge of the agencies in the community that serve or help children and parents.

Asking to take parenting classes before a baby is born is responsible, whether you're the mom or the dad!

Ask yourself the questions below ***before*** you talk to your support team. Here is a list of questions to find out your strengths and weaknesses:

- Is it easy for you to remember to schedule your own disability van rides?
- After you have scheduled the van ride, is it easy for you to be ready to go when your ride shows up?
- Is it easy for you to remember to call and cancel your ride if you won't be going?
- Is it easy for you to remember to make your child's and your doctor appointments?
- Is it easy to remember to go to your child's and your doctor appointments?
- Is it easy for you to remember to cancel doctor appointments if you are unable to go?
- Do you believe there are times when you are allowed to cancel a doctor appointment?
- If so, when is it okay?
- If not, why not?
- In what amount of time do you have to cancel an appointment? (Every doctor's office has different rules regarding cancellation and rescheduling.)

145

The reason these questions are so important is that when it comes to a child and their medical appointments, the professionals working for and around you need and want to make sure you can and will do everything your child needs to be done.

By showing them that you know the right thing to do, your doctor, counselor, and other healthcare professionals will be your best advocates!

If you are considering finding a partner who would be a good parent to your children, consider asking yourself the following questions:

- Do they have a job? (Do you have a job?)
- How much money do they make a month? (How much do you make a month?)
- How much money do they save a month? (How much money do you save a month?)
- How much money do they spend every month on their required bills? (How much money do you spend every month on required bills?)
- How much money do they spend on having fun every month? (How much money do you spend on having fun every month?)
- Do they want children? (Do you want children?)

You two would need to talk over how you will pay for the children if and when they come into the picture. These are possible suggestions:

- If only one person is working, can the second person get a job?
- Cut your spending. You can do this by cutting some of your bills (i.e., getting a cheaper cable or dish plan, cheaper cell phone plan, or spend less for other things).
- If both of you already have one job, are either of you willing to get a second job?

Look at yourself physically, emotionally, and your thinking ability for short and long range.

- What are your strengths and abilities?
- What are your weaknesses that are not your disabilities?
- What are your weaknesses that are because of your disabilities?

The weaknesses that are not disabilities will be easier to correct. The weaknesses that are caused by disabilities are going to be more difficult to make stronger, but this is where making accommodations or compromising works best! An example of a compromise: people who are deaf learning to read lips. An example of an accommodation: people who are deaf having a sign language interpreter and equipment that would help, such as a flashing light for the doorbell and phone.

Physically:

- Can you walk?
- Can you use your arms?
- Can you use your wrists?
- Can you use your fingers and fine motor skills?

If you have any problems with any of the above things, how do you accommodate your weaknesses?

If you are really strong, you need to be careful so you won't hurt a child accidentally! Adults have more strength than newborn babies do! Adults are taller and heavier.

Emotionally:

- Do you get easily stressed out?
- How often?
- What do you do to calm yourself down?
- Do you have anxiety attacks?
- How do you reduce your stress and anxiety?

147

- Do you hear voices?
- If so, how do you recognize the real world from the voices?
- Do you have mood swings?
- If so, how severe are the mood swings?
- If so, how do you handle mood swings?
- How do you deal with negative feelings such as being depressed, etc.?
- How do you handle your anger?
- How do you handle other's anger?
- When you are having emotional problems, how will you keep your children safe?

Mental or thinking ability:

- How often do you remember important things that people tell you?
- How easy is it for you to take notes?
- Do you remember to write appointments on the calendar?
- How do you look up addresses and phone numbers?
- Are you a fast thinker? For example, if the phone rings at the same time someone knocks on the door and you are cooking, in what order would you take care of everything?
- Can you tell the difference between medical problems that can be handled at home, ones that should be taken to minor emergency, or those that need to be handled at the hospital?
- If not, do you have friends or family members you can call and ask when something is medically wrong?
- Do you know how to keep from burning yourself?
- If you burn yourself, what would you do? Burn accidents *can happen to anyone*! How you handle any accident is very important.
- Do you know how to prevent accidents?

- Are you a self-starter or do you need someone to take you through every step until something is completed?

TO BOTH OF YOU: If you still want to be a parent, I would recommend strengthening one weakness at a time!

- Talk to someone regarding money issues about children.
- Talk to your support team about all the things you and your four friends talked over, including plans for how to strengthen your weaknesses or work with them or around them.

You and your support team can each pick out one or two weaknesses for you to work on. After your support team listens to you, it would be very smart to let them tell you which one or two they think would be the best for you to work on at this time so you can be a better parent, and let your support team know which one you want to work on. Talk it over and the two of you can choose which one you are going to work on, and if your support team thinks you can strengthen two weaknesses at the same time, then work on two.

*When you are ready to have a child or children, it is time to go see all of your doctors.

**Remember, life can quickly change. It's always smart to have one or more backup plans in case of an emergency. Emergencies just happen! They are never planned!

Finally, it's okay to wait to have children! Some people wait until:

- They are married.
- They are financially stable.
- They have finished college.

In fact, some people choose to finish college before they get married. I went to college while I was single, while I was engaged, and while I was married *with* children. From experience, I can tell you it is much easier to concentrate on college without children around.

Think carefully before you choose to have children. Having children is a lifetime commitment. Once you are pregnant or you have adopted a child, there is no backing out, even if your health goes bad or you have money problems in the future!

Long Distance Traveling

As you read the parts where people have traveled, consider:

- Did the person make plans before they traveled?
- Did they choose to travel with little or no planning?
- Did someone in the house have vacation time?
- Did someone in the house have to take time off work?
- Is anyone going on the trip with you? If so, does everyone who goes on the trip plan to share the cost? The more people that share in the cost, the cheaper it is, so everyone will have more spending money.

In 1993, I went to Sacramento with a man I was not married to. We went for religious reasons. We both saved enough money for our own "round trip" bus ticket.

Round trip means going somewhere and coming back home. We had saved money to eat at restaurants. We cut costs by sometimes going to a sit-down restaurant, buying one plate of food, and sharing the cost and the food. This was our main way of sharing expenses. Due to my religious and personal values, we never shared a motel room. I brought enough money to pay for my own room. This man was very angry with my boundary. He didn't bring enough money. He argued with me in front of other people, trying to get me to change my mind; however, I made him respect my boundary!

It would have been smart to have taken a little extra money in case there was an emergency. Possible emergencies that could have happened:

- A bus could have gotten stuck between home and Sacramento.
- There could have been a family emergency.
- Taxi fare, in case the bus stopped running.
- Hotel or motel money for an extra night if you can't get home.

151

I was too young to realize anything could have gone wrong. At age 22, I expected perfect weather in Sacramento, since I grew up in the snow and ice and always heard about sunny California.

In the future, I would probably never leave town with a man that I'm not married to unless my parents approve. However, I *chose* to travel with this man and **God protected me**! I was already very cautious because he was already trying to get me to do things I didn't want to do at home! Because he was trying to get me to do things I didn't want to, *I should have never left town with him*!

In 1994, I went to Olympia, the Washington State capitol. This is the city where legislators, senators and the governor meet to make, modify or repeal laws. I wanted to go talk to my State senator and representatives.

A group of people with disabilities went with an agency together to advocate for people with many kinds of disabilities. They took as many people with disabilities from the community as they could, along with as many employees as they had to for our health and safety. Caregivers, family members, and anyone else interested in helping advocate for people with disabilities were welcome to come. Everyone could advocate for themselves by telling many politicians about a part of their life and how a social service program helps them in their daily life. There were many agencies that serve the disabled population who went to Olympia that day.

It was called advocacy day and it was only for the day, so there were no motel costs. The agency I went with paid for everyone's airplane ticket, but everybody had to pay for their own food.

I still didn't know the importance of having extra money in case of an emergency. Since I was with a group and under the watchful eyes of the agency, I felt safe that the agency would have gotten me out of trouble if there was any trouble.

In 1994, I went back to Sacramento on the Greyhound bus. I went for the same religious reason as I did in 1993. My mom and I made plans for me to meet a woman in Pasco, Washington who was also going to Sacramento. I rode alone on the bus until I got to Pasco, and then she joined me. When she got on the bus, we rode the bus and we got a motel room together for our safety. We split the cost of the motel room.

In 1995, two of my friends and I got on a Greyhound bus and went to Tacoma, Washington for the same religious reason that I had gone to Sacramento. My bus ticket to Tacoma was cheaper than going to Sacramento because Tacoma was closer than California.

I saved enough money to pay for my own room because both of my friends smoked. One friend chose to smoke in the room and my other friend chose to smoke outside.

Remember earlier when I talked about setting your own boundaries regarding what is acceptable? My boundary was nobody was going to smoke in my motel room. I chose to share a motel room with the outside smoker. The other friend got her own room.

Since all three of us were on a strict budget, we looked for a motel that was reasonably priced, in a safe area, and close to the arena. We searched until we all agreed on one. Anytime we left the motel, we stayed together!

I took my next trip in 1998, and I was still single. (I will talk about my friend's trip later in this chapter.) The main thing to know is he took a trip up to meet my parents before I went down there. All seven days were a birthday present from my parents and friend. My parents bought my round-trip ticket to California. My friend paid for my stay in a motel room because we wanted to be under different roofs at night. Why? He wanted his privacy at night and I had only seen him face-to face one time. The other reason was my religious beliefs.

When I got off the airplane, he was there to greet me. He got me checked into my motel room. We drove around the Pacific Coast Highway. While driving around on the highway, I got to see the Pacific Ocean. Later that day, we went to the Chamber of Commerce. The Chamber of Commerce gives out information to promote the town and its businesses. There is also a section for visitors who want to know about the tourist attractions.

The second day, we went to Universal Studios. Universal Studios makes television shows and movies. We watched an animal show and got teased by Charlie Chaplin. Charlie teased me by tickling me with a straw of hay. He teased everyone he could! He did this to make the crowd laugh. He also dressed up funny. We got taken around by a tour guide. He showed us movie and TV show sets that had been made in the past and that were currently being made at the time I visited.

While visiting in 1998, I noticed Randy made a lot of U-turns. It looked like California and Washington driving laws were different. So, we went and got the California and Washington driver's guides to compare laws. I also got to meet his family.

Just about everyone in Washington I know wants to go to Disneyland and he took me there. I hated it! The lines were too long! We stood for so long my feet hurt and I got too tired! I just wanted to sit down or lay down! I wished I'd had a wheelchair while at Disneyland! We went driving around and to his apartment to rest. I got to see his large model airplane. We went and visited with a Christian family in his apartment complex and I met his landlord.

Day five, we went to Olivera Street. Olivera Street is a street where people sell Mexican things. This was very interesting to me. This is one time in my life I was glad to have someone with me because I don't know Spanish and was in an unfamiliar place. Later that day, we went and hung out at the motel, looked at all the different shops, and sat in the lobby.

On day six, we went to the Reagan Museum to see all the good and the bad things done while Ronald Reagan was an actor, the Governor of California, and the President of the United States, along with some of the things that have happened to the Reagan family in their personal lives. I remember the work he had done regarding tearing down the Berlin Wall. The Berlin

Wall was torn down one year after he was out of office. Nancy Regan had a program called *Just Say No to Drugs*. They also had things in a museum about Alzheimer's disease. Alzheimer's disease is a disease that President Reagan got after he was out of office. There are medications for Alzheimer's, but no definite cure for it at this time. They have information about other illnesses and diseases that someone in their family has had or has. They also had quilts hanging up on the walls in one room of the museum. Later on, we went to a small airport and went flying for two hours in a 110 Cessna. A 110 Cessna is a small airplane.

Day seven was my last day in California, so I checked out of the motel and put my things in my friend's car for the day. Then we headed off to Warner Brothers. Warner Brothers makes TV shows and movies, just like Universal Studios does. Warner Brothers made a show that I loved to watch. While at Warner Brothers, I got to see the car that was always jumping over things that were blocking the road such as water, a cliff or a dead end. After we left Warner Brothers, we drove by a place I would have been interested in working at if I had moved to California. During the seven days I was there, my friend took me out to eat and bought all my meals. My favorite place to eat was Sizzler. We went there as many times as possible because there were no Sizzlers in my hometown. We also went to other restaurants. My friend paid for my meals as part of my birthday present. Finally, he took me to the airport and got me on the plane. My mom was waiting for me at the airport and she brought me home.

In 2000, my fiancé's father had a stroke. I got a credit card with a fixed rate. Ask your support team what a fixed rate and a variable rate is. My parents disapproved. Their opinion was if you don't have enough cash, don't buy it!

However, my parents approved of the man I wanted to leave town with and understood that there was a possibility that this might be his last chance to see his father alive. It was important to me to give him emotional support, so I got a credit card anyway, so I could go.

Three months earlier, I had an emotional breakdown, and he was there emotionally for me, so my parents provided me with a calling card so I could be there for Eli. It was cheaper than using my cell phone! The reason my parents provided me with a calling card is so I could keep myself emotionally calm so I could be emotionally stable for Eli.

In 2002, we went to Hawaii for our honeymoon for eight days and seven nights. Since we were older and living alone before we got married, we received a lot of cash gifts for our honeymoon. Both of us were good at saving our money, so when we chose to get married, the money we saved in our own accounts and cash gifts were spent on our honeymoon.

We went to an island that had public transportation, so we didn't have to get a cab unless we wanted to! We had money to buy souvenirs to show that we really went to Hawaii. We sent some people postcards, we bought flowers that you wear around your neck, and we bought a photo album with the seven islands of Hawaii on the front cover. We went to Waikiki Beach and on a dinner cruise around Diamond Head. (If you get seasick, you would not like a cruise! It will make you sick!) It was fun in our opinion, but because of the waves, I had no balance! We also went to a restaurant on the 23rd floor called Top of Waikiki. It spins like the Space Needle in Seattle, Washington. We saw an Elvis impersonator who was very down-to-earth. We flew around Hawaii in a little airplane. We got to visit Honolulu, the capitol of Hawaii. A tour guide took us around and he took us to the Governor's office. Anyone on the tour who wanted to sit behind the Governor's desk and pretend to sign a bill got to. I chose to. My bill was titled *Disability Rights*.

We also went to hear S.O.S. sing. They are a group of seven men dressed up in funny costumes. They change their singers every once in a while. We also went to a luau and got pictures of a lighthouse while we were there.

Part of the motel cost was getting breakfast every morning. Every morning, we went down and got a "free" breakfast. We

156

ate breakfast there every morning except one. That morning, we had breakfast delivered to our room.

Our children didn't come with us. Eli's family watched them while we were on our honeymoon. By having our family watch them, we did not have to pay for childcare. When we went to Eli's 35th class reunion, his family handed our boys back to us. While at the 35th class reunion, we stayed in a motel room with two queen-sized beds. Our boys slept in one bed while Eli and I slept in the other. (To save money, if you only need one bed, check to see if a one bed room is cheaper than a two bed room!)

Eli also took me on a tour around the town where he used to live. He showed me places that were special to him. One place I was shown was called the big house which was three floors high. Eli did a lot of remodeling to the big house in the late 1980's and early 1990's. We also went to his favorite restaurant.

In reading about the next two vacations, look for the emergencies:

- Did they have to use their emergency fund? An emergency fund is money you don't plan on spending on your trip but will spend if you need to!
- If there was a crisis and they didn't use their emergency fund, what did they do? If you can't answer this question, it would be smart to accept help from your support team to find out what an emergency fund is and how it works.

Christmas 2003, Eli and I went back to see his parents. We let our grandson, who was the only child living at home, stay with another family member. This was the first time we had taken a trip when Eli was out of work, but maybe the last time we would see his dad alive. His dad was in his early 80's.

To save money and to spend time with Eli's best friend and college roommate he had met 25-30 years earlier, Eli wanted to stay with his friend. I did not! I almost stayed home because I thought it was unsafe. I just had a feeling that Eli's friend had no morals because Eli had told me things he did when they were in college. I was unable to explain why I felt so uncomfortable. I just did. Eli hadn't seen this man for 25-30 years and everything Eli had said about him sounded dangerous!

When both of them were single, if a woman wanted to date the roommate, it was accepted and understood by both men that the lady could choose which roommate she wanted. Eli had the opinion that women have their own mind and Eli was never going to force a woman to stay with him if she wanted to go out with his roommate. However, Eli's roommate treated women very differently. He treated women as if they were only here on earth for a man's pleasure. He didn't think he should have to think about a woman's needs, wants, desires, wishes, or feelings. This is how Eli talked about him and I had no proof that he had changed!

Eli thought his friend would respect his marriage vows. Eli was wrong, surprised, and angry to find out that he had to tell him that there were new boundaries by saying, "My wife is off limits!" I told Eli how this man violated me many times.

We spent the rest of Christmas vacation at Eli's parents' house. When we got home, Eli confronted him by e-mail and broke off their friendship! Eli trusts me more after going through that experience.

We would have had to stay somewhere else even if this guy was nice. The reason: I was having medical problems from his house being too cold. It was too cold because he turned down the heat and he kept his hot water tank off to save money!

MY FRIEND'S TRIP

My friend from California came to visit me in January 1998. On his way home, he hit black ice at 80-90 miles outside of the town I lived in. He crashed his car against a wall of rocks crushing his back window. No one was sitting in the backseat when the car accident happened. Someone called the State patrol on their cell phone. They helped my friend and gave him a ride to the nearest gas station. My friend called my parents to see if they could pick him up and bring him back. My parents were home, had no other plans and they had the money to get gas. My parents came to pick me up, get gas, and we went to pick him up. We took him to the airport. He bought his airline ticket. We stayed with him until he got on the plane. He used his emergency money to buy an airline ticket.

TO CHOICE MAKER: Save money for all the things you need by asking yourself these questions when planning for a trip:

1) Where are you going? Why are you going there?
2) How are you going to get there?
3) Where are you going to sleep? How many nights do you plan on sleeping in a hotel or motel? The days of the week and the dates are important, especially if you're traveling during a holiday!
4) Where will you eat all of your meals?
5) How are you going to get around town?
6) How much spending money do you want to take? You might want to buy things that are special to that area. (For example, when we went to Seattle, we went to the Space Needle. We bought a coffee cup and a water bottle shaped like the Space Needle. When we went to Hawaii, I brought back a whole bunch of leis.)
7) Emergency fund – How much money do you think you need to put aside in case of an emergency?
8) How many days will you be at your destination?

Here's another group of questions that will help you plan for a trip. These include making plans to leave and getting emotional support while you are gone:

1) If you have kids in school or when members of family works, you need to plan your vacations around everyone's schedule. Vacation time for children is called spring break, Christmas break, or summer vacation. Children also have three-day weekends throughout the

school year due to holidays. Sometimes, people have to take a leave of absence.

Leave of absence is taking time off from work without being paid for being gone. A person usually gets paid for vacation time, but they don't get paid for a leave of absence.

2) Do you need to put a hold on the newspaper and mail while you are gone, or have someone get it for you?

3) Do you need or want someone to take care of your house, pets, plants, etc. while you are gone? If you need someone to help you, there are three choices! Choose one of them so your home, pets, and/or plants will be taken care of when you are gone!

A) Get a house sitter. A house sitter is someone who lives in your home while you are out of town and will leave when you get home! While they are staying at your home, they will pick up your mail and newspaper every day. They will also take care of your pets and plants. Your home should look as clean as it was when you left! The benefit of having someone stay in your home while you're gone is to keep the robbers away! *Be sure you choose someone you trust 100% to have a key to your home!* If anything is missing, it would be easy to accuse your house sitter of stealing when you might have misplaced what you were looking for, meaning you found it later.

B) Have someone come to your home 1-2 times a day and check on everything. In the morning, they need to get your newspaper and feed your pets. Later on that day, possibly at nighttime, they need to come back to get the mail, water the plants, and see if the pets still have enough food and water until they come back in the morning. If you choose A or B, you'll have to trust the person you choose to watch your home because they will need a key temporarily until you are back in town.

C) The last choice would be to have your pets and plants taken care of at a friend's house until you come home! Put a hold on your mail and newspaper! A 'hold' temporarily stops the mail and newspaper until you ask them to start sending it again. Remember to take the hold off when you come home! Make a list of things you need so you remember everything.

Keep your medicines WITH YOU AT ALL TIMES, so if your luggage gets lost, you can still take your medicines! If you are taking a plane, bus, train, or boat, remember your ticket! Put the ticket in your wallet or purse!

Plan how much money you think you will need to cover the cost of the first set of questions related to money.

1) Do you have enough medicine to last you through your trip without having to go to a pharmacy?
2) Do you need or want any help from family or friends? (Examples would be, I let my mom purchase my plane tickets through the computer because she can find the best prices. Buying over the internet is cheaper but is more financially dangerous. I will never give my credit card information on the internet.) Another thing is, needing help packing. Packing is difficult for me, so I let people help me.
3) Do you need to have any emotional support from family or friends? (For example, on one trip I took, my parents gave me extra emotional support by giving me a calling card for the trip.)

I would strongly encourage you to talk to five people on your support team about your plans, so you don't have any bad surprises. One or two of them should be people who share your values. Some people might choose friends in Alcoholics

161

Anonymous. A second person could be your best friend, your third and fourth people should be one man and one woman that you trust who has been to the place you want to go to.

If you are unable to find anyone who have been where you want to go to, ask one close male and one close female friend who knows the most about where you want to go the same questions you would have asked the two people who had traveled there.

The reason to talk to people who share your values is so they can help you stick to your boundaries while you are on vacation when your personal and professional support team isn't with you.

The reason for choosing a close man and a close woman friend who have been where you want to go is, in different cities and states, people behave differently than in other cities and states. For example, if you plan on going to Salt Lake, Utah, you need to know that most people in Utah share a specific religious value. Why is this important to know? To prevent you from embarrassing yourself by making an inappropriate remark or joking about that religion! If you make a bad comment, most of the city might be mad at you.

No matter where I go, I would want to know from both men and women:

- What is the crime rate?
- How much crime is there against women and children?
- What are the most common crimes there?
- Are the people there friendly or do they keep to themselves? Is it slow or fast paced, etc.?
- What's the weather like there?
- What kind of clothes should I pack?

Men and women can help first time travelers know what to expect. I have learned that every airport I have been to does their security screenings differently. Some are rude. Some could have injured a person with a disability because they didn't know what they were doing!

Set up a time to talk to your support team that fits both of your schedules! This should put them in a better mood so they will have time to listen to you.

You should be able to say everything you want to, nicely without being interrupted until you are done talking. If your support team is quiet the whole time you are talking, you should give them the *same respect*! Be quiet and listen to them until they are done telling you their concerns! Even if they talk when you are talking, **don't** talk when it's their turn. Give them the respect you want!

Tell your support team everything you know about where you want to go and what you have learned. These could be things like:

- Ways to stay healthy (i.e., everything related to medicine, etc.).
- How are you going to keep yourself safe?
- Tell them who you talked to and why if you need to.
- Tell them how much money you have for the trip
- Tell them how much money you have budgeted out for food, hotel, transportation, emergencies, etc.
- Calling them and letting them know that you will call is a smart idea. (This shows that you are thinking of them.) Don't tell them this if you don't plan to. Be honest with them!

After both of you have heard everything each other has to say, then have a question and answer time.

TO SUPPORT TEAM: Let the choice maker tell you what they know and have learned about where they want to go. Tell them your personal experiences such as if/when you had to travel out of town for your job, vacation, and/or family emergency reasons. Tell them any difficulties you had regarding traveling. For example, if there's a family emergency, if you

163

have a job, you would have to explain to your boss what has happened, take any extra money that you were saving and spend it where you didn't plan to.

Also, if you, as part of the support team, still have things that concern you, tell them. Ask them any question you have so you won't be as worried. Let the choice maker give you all the answers they currently have and allow them as much time as they need to look up the answers for themselves and to see if they can answer your questions to be more independent instead of having you tell them they can't do something.

All the money questions in this chapter should help the choice maker know if they can afford to travel without being told they can't afford to go.

Let them find the answers for themselves whether that is through the internet, over the telephone, or asking anyone they choose to ask. They may ask their best friend, a brother/sister, a rabbi/pastor, or you. However, who they ask should be their choice.

Waiting until they ask you for help builds up their independence. Therefore, help them only when they request your help. Independence in this sentence means how much information they can find on their own. Another meaning of independence here is how much a person can look up or do before needing help. This includes knowing when to ask, what questions to ask and who to ask.

TO BOTH OF YOU: **Let them be as independent as they are comfortable with.** Therefore, step in only when they ask for your help.

Protecting Yourself in General

Here is a list of terms for this chapter. Read through what these words and phrases mean two or three times before you continue reading! It is very important to understand these words and phrases!

"Knowledge" is facts. Facts = knowledge.

"Understanding" is knowing why you make the choices you make.

"Experience" means things you have done before that will help you make choices in the future.

"Good choices" are healthy choices made without experience.

"Wise choices" are healthy choices made with experience.

When you get educated about something before making a choice, you are making an informed choice!

Through my job, I learned how to ask the right questions to get the answers I needed from businesses before I make choices. Why? I used to have a job doing telephone surveys.

"Right choice" means doing things that are smart, healthy or safe.

There are "foolish choices," "bad choices," and "wrong choices." Sometimes, it is okay to make a foolish, a bad or even a wrong choice depending on what it is! Why? If you never make a foolish, bad or wrong choice, you will *never* learn from them. Hopefully, you **will learn** from your mistakes when you make mistakes and won't keep making the same mistakes. There are some mistakes society won't let people make because the risk is too dangerous for your health and safety!!

The only way I agree with the intellectual disabled population making any foolish, bad or wrong choices is after they have been *informed* three times. If they are still making foolish, bad or wrong choices, then that's okay.

"Informed consent" or informed choice is when someone lets you know what could or will happen if you make that choice.

Informing someone can be done in writing. For example, I signed a two-year contract that said, "If I break this contract, I will have to pay them $200." Another example of informed consent is educating a child about his/her responsibilities if the parent buys him/her a pet.

With all the information people gather from every possible source, **people are informed**! Hopefully, the information will help them make better choices.

"Foolish" means lacking the knowledge and experience to make a smart choice. A person could lack knowledge if they are young. Anybody who ignores the advice of someone who has more knowledge than them is foolish!

Everyone starts out with no experience. However, each time you do something, you gain experience.

If the person *got the information explained to them* three **different times** and keeps insisting on doing it their way, **then let them** do it. The choice maker should be held legally responsible, not the support team. The person should get the credit for the good or bad choices they make!

They need to learn to take responsibility for their choices, good or bad!

"Bad choice" is a choice that was made because you didn't know what would happen. Either you didn't know or you were *still learning*. A bad choice, depending on how much knowledge you had, could be the choice to smoke. Why? Because you understand it stinks, but you also have friends that smoke. So, without thinking about anything else, you chose to smoke. If you had asked for more information, it would be a foolish choice. (Doing things only because your friends choose to, makes it a bad or foolish choice based on that reason alone.) If you had all the information, you would be making an "informed choice, whether the choice is good or bad!"

"Wrong choices" are things that are against the law or because it puts someone else in a very unhealthy and/or very unsafe situation. For example, I would do everything I could to stop my family and friends from taking illegal drugs because it's against the law, is unhealthy and unsafe.

Giving your bank account and social security number to people over the phone or over the computer is very unsafe and bad because it can hurt you financially. It puts your money in danger of being stolen electronically, and that's what makes it bad! A person who gives their social security number and/or their bank account number to a person who is not at work has a higher risk of having their money stolen!

Even if you start out making poor/bad choices you can learn to make better choices. Ask your support team to help you make better choices and help you understand different choices. **You** should be the one choosing who is on your support team. This team would be the ones to help you see things in different ways, but they should allow you to make up your own mind unless you want them to make a choice for you!

The ideas in the rest of this chapter come from a couple of different people. I use **most** of these ideas to protect myself. However, the ideas I don't use are still good ideas!

Choices could depend on your lifestyle as a whole and your ability to pay for it. For example, because of my lifestyle, I should have a cell phone because I stay out until it is dark and I ride the disability van by myself.

The following are health and/or safety reasons to have a cell phone. If you:

- Get home after it is dark
- Have health problems
- Are out in public alone
- Have children
- Easily get lost

I wrote about cell phones in an earlier chapter.

The next part is written for the people who want to live in an adult family home, group home, etc., but who also want to go out in the community without a caregiver. These people just want their caregivers 'at the house'! At other times, a resident may want the caregiver to be with them when they are out in the community.

(The problem I have noticed is the support team forces people with disabilities to receive services/things that he/she does not want or would like to learn to live without!)

When it's possible, go out in a group of two or more because there's safety in numbers, but it is not always possible.

What to say when you meet someone new:

- Greet them by saying, "Hi."
- Make "small talk" with new people.
- Check their body language.
- Did they smile, or look away, or down?
- Did they say anything to you?
- If so, what did they say?
- You have to decide from what they say and their body language if they want to continue talking or not.

If they want to talk, here are some safe topics to talk about until you get to know each other better. You can talk about the place where you met, sports, weather, music, news, food, college, or employment.

How long you have known someone, where you know them from, and who you are with depends on what would be good subjects to talk about and what subjects should be avoided.

Get the other person to talk about a subject and then share your thoughts about the same subject.

*Don't try to get to know everything about someone and no one should try to get to know everything about you.

Here are some unsafe topics when you first meet someone: religion and politics should be off limits. You can choose to bring up the subjects after getting to know the other person a little bit. The exception would be if you meet at a religious or political function or organization. If that's where you met them, then those subjects should be okay to talk about.

Other unsafe topics: If there is a subject that bothers you or the other person, don't talk about that subject to *that person*. It may rub you or them the wrong way.

Here is an example: I get irritated with the door-to-door style of getting a religious message because I'm happy with my faith. However, I like to know what other people's faith is and watch their faith in action so if I'm upset with my religion, I can watch other's and see if their lives are better and happier or see that it's not working for them. This is a kind of research I do to make an informed choice. As for now, *I am happy with my faith.* I don't want people at my door telling me I will be happier with a different religion! I also don't want salespeople at my door! I don't need the new service or new product that door-to-door salespeople are selling. When it comes to buying something, I want to shop around for it myself! I need my home to be peaceful and safe from door-to-door missionaries and salespeople. I have nothing against people of other religions or salespeople as long as that's not their reason for knocking on my door! If I buy what salespeople want me to buy, I won't have enough money to buy the things I need or want. That's why I don't want them at my door or in my home!

Keeping quiet about things that one person has a strong opinion about lowers the chances of angering each other!

Neither one of you should be sharing each other's problems because it can lead to advice giving or asking for advice. These people are not part of your "support team." Neither one of you knows each other well enough to give each other advice. The only people who should give you advice are your professional and personal support team!

- Never make personal remarks about someone's looks.
- Never gossip.
- Never lie about anybody.

169

Lying about someone can hurt someone's reputation, and that could hurt their life.

A good test to know if you are gossiping or in a conversation where others are gossiping is, would you like those things said about you when you are not around? If your answer is no, avoid saying those things when the person is not there!

- Never complain.
- Never flirt with people you don't know!

Get to know them before choosing if they are safe unless you are in immediate danger!

*It is wrong to ask or be asked, "How much money do you make?" or "When do you get paid?" *Beware* of answering the next question, "What day of the week do you get paid?" If you answer this question honestly, you make it very easy for people to take financial advantage of you. If you tell someone the answers to money questions, they might ask you for money on payday or you put yourself in more danger of someone stealing your money or your paycheck. If you give them your bank account number, they could take money out of your account electronically and you would not know until it's too late.

Unsafe Behaviors

- Borrowing or lending money or things of high personal or dollar value.
- Accepting rides from strangers.
- Accepting or asking for favors from strangers.

TO BE SAFE:

- Know your surroundings.
- Walk with your head up and shoulder's back.
- Walk as if you know where you are going.
- Walk like you must get somewhere!

- Never show fear.
- Stay true to your boundaries!

Remember, you set the boundaries with the help of your support team. You choose which family members and friends are allowed to be on your support team. Trust them to protect you if and when your boundaries are violated! Trust them to help you enforce your boundaries, so it will be difficult for anyone to break them!

Tell your support team what your boundaries are and why those are *your* boundaries. If your support team disagrees with your boundaries, you may need or want to explain your reason(s) for your choice(s). You can ask them to help you set some of your boundaries!

Who you choose to be around can protect you or put you in danger.

Everyone needs to protect their health!

Depending on the kind of person you are or want to be, people may see you as a safe or dangerous person. People may see you as a person to be friends with or to avoid.

For the first three years, it may be a smart idea to have your support team help you to know who is safe, unsafe or neutral.

*USE CAUTION AT ALL TIMES: If anyone is physically bothering you in the community, here are four more things you can do to protect yourself:

- Take a self-defense class.

Someone who wants to hurt you doesn't care if you have a disability, but you need to use your abilities and accommodate your disabilities to protect yourself *if* you are being attacked!

- Get a cell phone even if it's only for emergencies!

There is one kind of phone call that the state and federal government says is free! The free phone call is for health and safety reasons. Ask your support team if having a cell phone would help you stay healthier and safer. If you have a cell phone, would your support team feel more comfortable with you living on your own or going out in public by yourself?

- If someone is bothering you, call the police.

The officer needs to know *who* is bothering you. They need to know what the person looks like. They will ask you if you know their name and any of their personal information like their address, e-mail address, etc. They will want your name, phone number, address, and e-mail address so the investigators can contact you.

- Get one or more of these items: mace, pepper spray, or a zapper.

You *only use* the device when you need to stop someone from physically or sexually hurting you!! Never use the above items if you are not in danger! I personally don't use a whistle because it is also a child's toy. I only want to use something that is used to get help. If I need help, I don't want there to be a mistake. I want someone to help me when I need it!!

- Know the time, and where your disability van or city bus will pick you up, especially in public!

If you live by yourself or have a roommate(s): You are responsible for yourself and they are responsible for themselves.
*These are ways of protecting your home:

- Keep your doors and windows closed and locked when you leave. Anyone can walk through the door! Anyone can tear off the screen from a window; however, it slows them down! This is why your windows should be closed and locked!
- Never go to sleep with the doors or windows open or unlocked at night! Chances are they will walk into your

home, and/or tear the screen off your window if you leave something unlocked. Again, locking them slows them down!
- Put timers on your lights so lights turn on and off in different rooms so it looks like you are home when you are gone!

Here's an example. The lights are on in the kitchen and get turned off in 45 minutes. A minute later, the living room lights turn on. You program the lights to be turned on and off in the same way you would do it when you are home.

How long does it take you to walk from one room to the next room? The answer is the amount of time it takes you to turn the light off in one room and the light on in the next room is how you program it. *It's about the safety of your home when you are gone.* This is so people will be less likely to break in because they think you are home when you're really gone!

If you own or are buying your home, you can get a security system.

Money Wise

All government social service workers who ask you for your social security number and/or bank information need it, but you might need or want someone on your support team with you until you learn how to double-check that someone really is who they say they are! If they prove that they really do work for a social service organization, give them all the information they ask for. First, make them prove they work there! How?

1) Make them show you their badge. It will show the name of the company they work for and their name.
2) If you are not sure, call the company and ask them if they have an employee by the name on that's on their badge.
3) If you have never met someone who is coming to your house, find out what they look like and what their car looks like. (If you've never met them, you may want to call the company just to make sure this person really works there.)

Things to look out for financially:

- A social service agency will never ask you for your Social Security number or bank information over the internet.
- They will usually have you bring information into the office or they will come to your house if they need financial information.
- Social service agencies can do phone interviews.
- Social service workers will tell you in advance before they send something in the mail for you to sign.

If you get something in the mail from your social service agency that only wants you to sign your name at the bottom and no one from the agency told you they were sending it, call them to find out if they sent you the letter! If they didn't, don't sign it and shred the letter!

- Face-to-face contact is best when doing business that involves signing a contract or sharing private financial information, including using your debit or credit card number.

If you can't buy something in person, then buying it over the phone is the next best choice. If buying online is the only way to buy something, I'd give my money to someone on my support team to buy it and have them give it to me.

- **Never** give your social security number, your credit card and/or bankcard number to anyone who is not at work!
- Communicate with your support team *before* you sign anything!

When you sign something, it is called a contract. You have to sign a contract to:

- Rent an apartment/home
- Buy a car
- Buy a cell phone
- Open a savings or checking account

*Contracts are legally binding! Signing a contract shows that you agree to everything that is written on the paper you signed. If you don't understand something, ask *before* you sign it. If you need to, ask if you can take it with you and show it to your support team.
*Keep a copy for yourself!
In my opinion, if you buy things with cash, you will have fewer money problems!

Car Safety Tips

When riding or driving in a vehicle, **lock the doors**! If the doors are left unlocked, anyone (i.e., a violent stranger) can come up, open the door, and do anything they want to.

When coming back to your car at night, use a flashlight and look under your car to be sure no one is hiding there.

When no one is in the vehicle, lock the door so no one can break in. They may want to steal the radio, something you bought from the store, the vehicle, or they might want to hurt you.

*No matter what a thief wants to steal, having your doors locked slows them down!

Resources in the Community

There are different resources for different things. When a person's car breaks down, they will go to the phonebook (a resource) or the internet (another resource) to find the right person to fix their car.

The customer who wants to use a "product" or "service" would be smart to ask questions of other customers who have used that business' products or services. The person who is looking to buy a product or a service would also be smart to ask the business questions. Some of the questions would be:

- How much does it cost?
- What does the product/service do?
- What is so good about their company?
- Ask any questions that you think would be important to make an informed choice.

A "product" is something that you buy. A "service" is something someone does for you like fixing a broken part on a car. In the restaurant business, food is the product being sold and the service is the waiter/waitress and cashiers serving you!

The kinds of resources that I'm writing about in this chapter are those that will help people who have disabilities be more independent.

Before I moved out of my parents' home, my mom got me connected with the Division of Vocational Rehabilitation (DVR). DVR got me in touch with another agency that taught me how to live independently.

One of the first skills I was taught was to ride the city bus. I wasn't always able to safely ride when I had to, so I was given paperwork to fill out and my doctor had to fill out part of it. Then I had to mail the form to the transportation company and wait. It took them two weeks to decide if I was eligible to ride the disability van. I was eligible, so when I can't ride the bus safely, I ride the van. I was taught how to schedule my own van rides.

177

TO CHOICE MAKER: If you can figure out how to travel around every day on the city bus or the disability van without any help, then your support team would be more likely to let you live on your own.

The agency taught me how to be assertive. Assertive people can tell others their needs and wants in a nice and firm way!

Some people are "passive." "Passive" means rarely or never telling others what they like, love, need, and want. Passive is also keeping your opinions to yourself and going along with the crowd **even when you should speak up**. An example of passive would be never telling others what you like to eat and never telling anyone what restaurant you would like to eat at.

The problem with that is, someone is always making choices for you and when something is very ***important to you***, you might not have the ability to say what you need to say! If you never speak up on the smaller issues, how are you going to speak up when something is important such as preventing someone from getting hurt?

Now that I know how to be assertive, I can never be passive when I have a need or a want.

Another example of being assertive is, when I planned my birthday party at a restaurant, I chose where to have it. However, I listened to my friends' opinions of where they would want to eat at. I made the final choice because it was *my* party! I chose a buffet style restaurant, so everyone could choose what they each wanted to eat.

There are also people who are "aggressive." "Aggressive" people tell other people what to do and say. They may even tell them when to do things. Aggressive people are very controlling because they want to get their own way. (If I'm not careful, I <u>can</u> come across as aggressive.) Aggressive people only care about themselves or come across as only caring about themselves!

Finally, there are "passive-aggressive" people. These people are quietly frustrated for a very long time without looking angry on the outside. Then suddenly they explode with anger on everyone! This cycle repeats itself of being frustrated for a long time, not showing their feelings, and exploding with anger all over again until this person learns new patterns to break the bad habit of hiding their feelings until they explode.

"New patterns" in this case means learning new ways, such as expressing frustration when it happens and speaking up for himself/herself, and by becoming nice and kind.

The goal of the agency that taught me these skills was to help people with disabilities learn how to live independently in a way that will help them avoid being a victim. It also teaches them how to get what they need or want without making someone else a victim.

If others in authority see that someone can't or refuses to speak up for himself/herself, that person might need a power of attorney or guardian. This should be the last option. A good power of attorney or guardian will take the time to get to know the person who they are speaking on behalf of!! A good power of attorney or guardian will also know what the person likes, dislikes, and hates and the reasons or possible reasons they feel that way. If a power of attorney or guardian must make a choice against a protected person's wishes, they need to at least know how the protected person thinks things through to make the next best choice!

The person needs to understand that if they have a power of attorney or guardian, they have legal requirements they must follow. At this time, their main legal requirement is to make sure that the person is kept healthy and safe. If the person dislikes the way(s) in which they are being kept healthy and safe, it's time to fight for what they believe in through the political system. This is done by contacting people who work in the government by making phone calls, writing/e-mailing letters, or going to their office. There are people who work for the county or city, people who work for the State, and others who serve the United States government (the country).

Some of my weakest skills are meal planning, cooking, and shopping for food. I don't know how to read nutrition facts on the back of labels or recipes very well. I physically have trouble standing on my feet and I have trouble working with both hands. I have a caregiver that helps me grocery shop, meal plan, read labels (when I ask her to), and cook.

I also have trouble with a few personal care tasks. Here is a short list of what personal care tasks are:

- Help walking
- Help taking a shower
- Help to get and take medicine(s)
- Help getting dressed
- Help someone transfer from bed to chair, etc.
- Help with teeth, hair, etc.

Everyone needs help at some time! To get this resource, a caseworker must approve it and tell the caregiver what they can and cannot do safely!

One agency tried to teach me all the skills related to cooking and keeping a house. However, I still had trouble physically cooking and cleaning house and remembering to wear gloves when cleaning so I was given a caregiver to do what I could not. I did learn some tasks, but I always got very tired after doing the tasks. So, even though I knew how to do the tasks mentally, physically I couldn't do anything for two days after doing some chores. I was given a caregiver and I gladly accepted the help!

It takes a long time to budget money well enough so that those who care about you will not be concerned about you financially. Nobody can learn how to properly manage money within one day or a week. People who are smart get advice from their support team. They can also read books, take classes, get information from the internet, etc.

It takes learning, discipline and practice to manage money correctly!

*If you have trouble budgeting, you can get a representative protective payee (a resource). The payee will make sure *all* of your required and optional bills are paid before you get your spending money. The payee will work with every client and their money to choose what day of the week, of every month that they will come in to get their money. The payee may give the client their money once a week, like every Thursday or the payee may give them spending money two times a month (like getting paid every two weeks) or might give them all their money for the month.

If I had trouble budgeting money, here are a few reasons I would **want** a payee *at first*! I'd want to learn how to manage my money as soon as possible *if that's possible*:

- Having a payee costs money.
- Paying for a payee is another bill.

However, it is better to have an extra bill and have someone manage my money, so I don't go into debt and lose everything I own. But I would want to learn to manage my money as soon as possible so I could have one less bill. That way, every month I could save or spend that extra money on something I want.

If someone fails to pay bills, they will lose services not paid for. Examples of this would be having the phone, electricity or cable shut off. Unpaid bills will result in services getting shut off or products getting taken away. If this happens, you will have bad credit!

Another problem I have with a payee is that I could only get my money at certain times, so when I wanted to buy something on sale, I couldn't get the money out even if it was a good deal for me because it was not my scheduled day to get money. (By managing my own money, I can go to the bank and get the money to buy what's on sale. I can also use my debit card.)

To help me or anyone else live as independently as possible, caseworkers can and will help their clients get assistive technology devices. Assistive technology devices can help people who have disabilities do more for themselves. Examples of assistive devices would be button hooks, easy open medicine bottles (which allow people with no use or very little use of their hands to dress themselves and take their own medicines), etc.

All in all, that agency taught me or tried to teach me how to be healthy.

Safety in cooking is for everyone's safety. For example, if you don't turn the stove off when you're done cooking, your neighborhood might burn down.

If you usually eat unhealthy food and rarely eat healthy food, your health is in danger!

(If you are physically challenged or have low stamina, it is to your benefit to ask for help with grocery shopping. This help could come from family, friends and caregivers.)

Keeping yourself clean is as important as keeping your house clean. This keeps germs from forming on your body which will keep you from getting sick. (This helps your physical health!) It is also important to stay clean because if you look dirty and smell bad, people will treat you bad. By keeping yourself clean, you might be protecting yourself from being teased.

Keeping your house clean is for everyone's safety and health because if your house gets too messy, your papers might get on the heaters or stove in the kitchen and catch your house on fire and a fire *can spread* to other houses.

There are different safety and health problems when the dishes are always dirty, the floors are rarely swept, or when the bathrooms or bedrooms are rarely dusted and vacuumed. (A house can be mildly cluttered with papers and clothes, but never cluttered with food!) The reason food can never be part of the clutter on the floor is ants and other bugs are attracted to it and that's very unhealthy.

My family will put food (like chicken bones) on the floor long enough for the cat to have the rest of the chicken, and then we pick up the bone(s), so the ants and other bugs will stay out of the house.

Advocating for yourself protects you from "being taken advantage of." "Being taken advantage of" means one person or an agency is not listening to or is being disrespectful to another person. The first person or agency keeps pushing until you give in and you say or do what they want you to say or do!

There is also what I call system advocacy. This is where many agencies help people who have many different kinds of disabilities stand together to protect everybody's services and rights so they can continue to be independent and increase their independence!

After all, if we as the disabled community lose our cash benefits, food-stamps, medical benefits, job coaches, transportation, etc., how would we survive?

There are also good safety and health reasons that you would want to be "disciplined" with your money. "Disciplined" means managing your money by spending only as much money as you have. Another definition of discipline is if you can't pay cash, **don't get it**.

Tell only the professionals who need to know about your money. This would be so businesspeople can find out if you can pay for something every month such as a cell phone, a house, a car, etc. Another group of people you must tell is people who work in the government that you are receiving services from and when applying for government help.

You *need* to know *all* your rights and responsibilities *before* you sign anything! If you tell your friends and family how much money you make, they might want you to give it or loan it to them. They might not pay you back. You will be kept financially safer in a couple of ways if no one knows how much money you have.

- First, if no one knows if you have money, fewer people will try to rob you.
- Second, fewer people will ask you for your money because they will think you have no money.
- Third, even when you do have money "on you," you still can't afford to hand out money if no one is paying you back! You can use your money just as much as everyone else can!

- Fourth, strong recommendation: Don't loan people money! Loaning money is what banks/credit unions are for!!

I tried to cover as many subjects as possible in this book, but none of them in very much detail. It is up to you to find out what your needs and wants are. My goal has been to provide you with a little information and questions in every chapter so you can make educated choices about how you live your life!

Most authors who write self-help books usually focus on one subject such as losing weight or managing money and they usually go into detail on how to do whatever subject they chose to write about. No matter what the subject is, it is smart to ask different people you trust for their help and opinions.

Is Guardianship Good or Bad and Do You Need or Want One?

**Anyone can get a:

- Advanced Directive (medical and mental health)
- Living Will
- Will
- Durable Power of Attorney and/or a Power of Attorney if guardianship has not yet been established!

**The following are less restrictive ways to remain safe:

- Advanced Directive
- Advocate
- Durable Power of Attorney
- Power of Attorney
- Trustee
- Will
- Living Will

The above list are all less restrictive ways to maintain as much independence as possible.

(If you need to know what an advanced directive is, ask a lawyer or a very knowledgeable person that you trust.)

Take reasonable health precautions!

Take responsibility for your own actions!

"Surrogate decision-maker" in this book means someone who makes the choices that a person needs and cannot make for himself/herself. The surrogate decision-maker can make choices for the incapacitated/incompetent person because they talked to each other about their wishes before they became incapacitated and/or incompetent.

"Guardianship" is a legal process to see if someone needs a guardian. The process of guardianship is done in court. It is a smart idea for the judge or jury to see and hear the person whom they are making the choice about.

As I teach you what some of the words or phrases mean, I will also take you through this legal process using easier language.

***This information is to be used as a guide!** If you have specific questions or an open legal case, talk to your lawyer! If you don't have a lawyer, get one!

"Representative" means someone who stands up for other people.

*Each State has different guardianship laws. Ask a lawyer if you need to know the guardianship laws in your State.

Since most people hate other people having all the control over their lives, a judge or jury will try to find the least amount of control needed! They will use the phrase "least restrictive alternative."

"Least restrictive alternative" means the judge or jury will look at all other options/choices such as a representative protective payee, an advocate, a trustee, or power of attorney before appointing a guardian. A guardian is looked at as the last choice!

"Judge" means one person who sits in the courtroom and decides court cases.

"Jury" means a group of people who decide a court case.

To the best of my understanding, the guardianship process gets started when someone applies to be a guardian over someone else. This takes place in Superior Court at the courthouse. A guardian ad litem is assigned by the court.

Here's what some of the above words or phrases mean:

"Proposed": When the word "proposed" is used *before* the words guardian, ward, protected person, or vulnerable person, "proposed" means the court case is **in the process** *of being decided*!

"Proposed ward" means it is not yet decided if this person needs protection or not. Two other ways of saying 'proposed ward' would be proposed protected person or proposed vulnerable person. ("Ward" and "ward of the State" are legal terms.)

"Guardian ad litem" (GAL): A guardian ad litem is a lawyer appointed by Superior Court. A GAL's job is to find out what is in the best interest of the proposed person. The GAL *must* get medical/mental health, behavioral, educational (IQ) records, and find out what the person's goals, likes/dislikes, etc. are. The GAL *must* talk to everyone involved in the protected person's life which include the proposed protected person, their caregiver's, the proposed guardian, close and extended family that have an interest in them, their friends and clergy (if they have clergy), etc. After looking at the overall safety and health of a person and doing all the interviews, the GAL's final job is to write a report to the judge or jury of what they think would be the safest, but least restrictive alternative before any kind of guardianship is considered! Sources: Guardianship Services of Seattle and National Guardianship Association Inc.

A GAL is a lawyer who might have human services skills, but human services skills is not a requirement of the job, therefore it is rare to find a GAL who has human services skills. If you know anything factual (including personality differences between a protected person and a guardian), report it to the GAL. Sources: Guardianship Services of Seattle and National Guardianship Association Inc.

"Interested person" means anyone in the community who has a concern for the proposed protected person. Interested people need to make their concern(s) known based only on facts! Make all concerns known to the GAL.

If there's a specific concern, tell the GAL the date(s) of specific problem(s), what happened at the time, and the results. They need to know every time this happens, what were the circumstances, and how long the problem has gone on. This helps the GAL keep everything straight in their head so the report(s) make sense to the judge or jury reading the report!

It would be very smart to go to their hearing! If it's your hearing, tell the people you want to be there. During the hearing, the judge or jury will make a decision of how competent/capacitated the proposed protected person is.

"Competence/competent person" means a person's thinking ability. How do they solve problems, make choices, and get things done? Competence is referring to a person's thinking ability to make judgments and choices!

"Incompetence/incompetent person" means the inability to think things through to make a choice and/or the inability to solve problems and mentally follow through with the necessary steps to accomplish things!

"Capacitated/capacitated person" is a legal term for a person who is physically able to take care of himself/herself. The judge or jury might not give them a guardian, but might look into assigning them an advocate, payee, trustee, etc. to assist them.

"Incapacitated/incapacitated person" is a legal term for a person who is physically unable to take care of themselves.

If a judge or jury decides that a proposed protected person *is* incapacitated and/or incompetent, the person will get a guardian if nothing else helps them.

At the end of a *hearing*, the judge or jury will decide if a person is:

- Competent or incompetent
- Capacitated or incapacitated

"Protected person" means the judge or jury has decided that the person is "incompetent" and/or "incapacitated," so the word "proposed" is dropped. When that decision has been made, they become a "protected person."

"Limited guardian" is a guardian that has partial control. There are many kinds of limited guardians. Contact a lawyer or your State capitol to find out what all the types of guardians are in your State. Each State is different.

There are two types of common limited guardians in the State of Washington:

- Guardian of the person
- Guardian of the estate

"Guardian of the person" means having power over the protected person's "person" meaning protecting their body medically and protecting them from abuse. How? The guardian of the person is in charge of talking to all the doctors, caregivers, pharmacies, etc. and is responsible for making sure *all* the medical professionals work together! I don't know how they protect them from abuse, but they are also there to protect them from anyone who has hurt them in the past, and to prevent them from getting hurt. I don't know if they have any other responsibilities. If they do, I don't know what they are!

"Guardian of the estate" has control over large amounts of money such as a house, car, truck, camper, property, stocks, bonds, etc.

A lawyer (including a free lawyer) can help the protected person know what they can do and what the guardian's job is.

There are a couple of other choices related to having control over a protected person's money. Other choices are a:

- Trustee
- Representative protective payee
- Financial power of attorney

"Bond" is a kind of insurance that protects the protected person's money and other property (i.e., car, house, and things that are expensive).

"Full guardian" has 100% responsibility for the protected person and that includes the requirement of talking to the protected person because they need to know the person's opinion. However, the guardian is 100% responsible for everything that happens to them.

If the guardian goes on a vacation, gets sick, is temporarily incapacitated, or dies, a standby guardian temporarily fills in. The standby guardian can apply to become a guardian when the original guardian is unable to do the job properly.

Anyone can apply to be a guardian, but the judge or jury will usually consider a family member or the standby guardian first.

"Standby guardian" is the guardian who legally takes over when the guardian is *unable* to do the job!

It is illegal and wrong for guardians to make choices based on the guardian's values, beliefs, goals, desires, needs, wants, etc. The guardian must make decisions based on the protected person's values, beliefs, goals, desires, needs, wants, etc.

Any concerned person can apply to be their guardian! The job requirements to be a guardian:

- Must be at least 18 years old
- Live in the same State as the protected person
- Have a sound mind
- Never have been convicted of a felony

On a legislative level, guardians are given two guidelines in the process of decision-making:

- "Substituted judgment"
- Looking out for the individual's "best interest!"

"Substituted judgment" occurs when a guardian finds out how the person made choices before the person became incompetent/incapacitated. The guardian must look at his/her overall lifestyle including their social, religious, political, multicultural, and economic background. They must look at *everything that is important* to them!

"The principle of substituted judgment is considered to be the manner in which the autonomy, values, beliefs, and preferences of the protected person are best protected." Source: National Guardianship Inc.

On the other hand, if a GAL is unable to find out anything about their values, goals, wants, desires, etc. or how they would make choices, then he/she will use the second guideline. This is called looking out for someone's "best interest."

"Best interest" means health and safety.

At the time, my only understanding of guardianship was when a guardian makes medical and mental health choices on behalf of a protected person so their medical condition stays the same or gets better. However, everyone should take care of their own health, whether they are disabled or not. Being healthy will cost the government less money.

In order for a guardian to make choices that would be closest to the protected person's personal choices, the guardian must learn as much as possible about the person they are representing so they will be able to respect their wishes with the exception of anything that puts a person's health or safety in danger. Health and safety are most people's two most important issues.

"Guardians may have to get advice from medical and financial professionals or from special ethics committees" in order to act in the best interest of their protected person.

My personal opinion is that having a guardian is an excellent idea for health and medical reasons **if you think** healthcare professionals will misunderstand or ignore you. If I thought any of my health care professionals were ignoring or misunderstanding me, I would get a medical power of attorney or guardian to talk to them for me or get a new doctor!

Guardians can be great when advocating for a second doctor's opinion when there is a disagreement over what to do or they can force *all* your doctors to work together!

**I saw a situation where a woman could talk, and she had no power of attorney and no guardian! She talked to her medical doctor, mental health professional, care giving agency, and caseworker who were *all* ignoring her. The healthcare professionals were not working together to meet her needs physically and emotionally. The result: she died!

If she had had a power of attorney or a guardian for medical and health reasons, every healthcare professional would have been legally answerable to her power of attorney or guardian when she was being misunderstood or was being ignored by her healthcare professionals!

Current laws in some states give guardians the right to choose where the protected person lives. In my opinion, a guardian needs to include the protected person's opinion, but the guardian must have the final say on healthcare issues when their choice is going to put their health in danger. A person must be living in what most people would consider 'safe housing' in order to choose where they live. The guardian should suggest housing options around their health and the protected person can let the guardian know if they have any wishes about their housing.

My personal choice was renting an apartment and having a caregiver come into my home for the first ten years. I lived alone and needed and wanted help. A couple of times, I ended up in the hospital and I got more hours. I chose to take *fewer* hours than my caseworker said I needed. I took what I needed! Each protected person (client) has a different amount of hours that they are eligible for. It is based on the individual's **needs**!

I have talked to a lot of people who have guardians and about half of the protected people who can talk and have told me they dislike a lot of the major choices that their guardians make. Almost all of the protected people who are unable to talk like their guardian's choices or they don't care what choices are made. (I assume they like the choices that are being made since they *can't* say if they don't!)

I have seen other responsibilities given to guardians other than for medical and healthcare reasons.

Basically, a protected person must get permission from their guardian before getting married or getting a divorce, voting or holding an elected office, or getting a driver's license. A protected person might also have to ask permission to make or revoke a will, or possibly any other kind of legal papers like a living will, to sue someone and to buy, sell or own property. Finally, a protected person *may need* to get permission to choose their friends.

All 50 **states have different laws**! I'm aware of some of Washington State's laws.

Some protected people I have met want to:

- Choose where they live
- Get married
- Get a cell phone
- Go on a vacation

To my understanding, the following doesn't fall under the guardianship laws, however, it may fall within everyday communication skills! (If something requires a financial contract, it might be a guardianship issue!)

In order to be more independent, a protected person should:

- Develop communication skills.
- Communicate to and with your support team about everything you would like to do yourself or learn to do yourself!
- Re-read the chapters in this book that discuss things you want to get better at.

"If a person does not have the ability to exercise a right, the person does not benefit by having that right!" (J. Eli Harvey)

There are two Washington State laws related to guardianship. ALL Washington State laws start with "RCW." "RCW" stands for Revised Code of Washington. The two laws are:

- RCW 11.88
- RCW 11.92

RCW 11.88 explains (to the best of my understanding):

- Who needs to have a guardian
- Why they need to have a guardian
- When the guardianship starts and ends
- How guardianship is put in place
- How long it lasts (short-term or long-term)

RCW 11.92 is the law that tells guardians about the policies, procedures, and all the paperwork they must do, and who the guardian must report to and how often.

WARNING! Many problems that arise are because the guardian ad litem's job is a legal job. A GAL is not required to have any humanitarian interpersonal skills!

GALs depends on everyone who knows and cares about the protected person to educate the GAL about them.

*In my opinion, GALs and guardians should be required to complete three classes related to communicating specifically with (proposed) protected people before they are allowed to be a GAL or a guardian.

When someone becomes a guardian, he/she should be required to meet with everyone who works with the protected person one time a year! The guardian should also have a "long meeting" with the person they represent to assess them to see if their needs, wants, wishes, goals, and/or desires have changed. Also, the guardian should check to see if any of his/her goals have been met. If there are goals that they haven't met, is it still a goal. This should be done in a relaxed way while doing something the protected person enjoys!

Mismatching a protected person with a guardian who ignores or misunderstands the protected person is extremely bad!!

A guardian ad litem must consider **all** the medical reports, but should also include the proposed protected person's strengths! However, an appointed guardian should rarely look at the weaknesses of a protected person. Except for medical and health choices, a guardian should always be looking for ways to help them not need them as much!

Even when the protected person is in agreement with having a guardian, I have witnessed that older protected people want more freedom. These freedoms could include:

- What type of job they have
- Where they attend college (for credit or not)
- Which kind of transportation they use

194

- Be married
- Have children

All of these wants requires social/interpersonal skills!

Your employer, family, friends, coworkers, guardian, and strangers all need to be communicated with in different ways. You need to learn how each person should be talked to. If you don't know, ask your support team!

My suggestion would be to see where people are at "maturity-wise" by asking different questions.

"Mature" or "maturity" means growing up, handling life, and gaining responsibility a little bit at a time. You gain maturity every day by the choices you make and your experiences. Check all areas of life on a person's 25th, 30th, 35th birthday, continuing every five years until the protected person no longer needs a guardian or is satisfied with the level of guardianship they have.

Questions could include:

- Is this guardian still the right person to serve as this person's guardian?
- Is there a need for a new guardian?
- Has the protected person learned some things so that the guardian can be less restrictive as he/she had been?
- Has the protected person learned enough skills that they do not need a guardian at all or only in fewer areas of their life?

Add in your own questions such as: Does the guardian and protected person have a personality conflict? Tell the GAL anything you think they should know when making a choice about the best match for the protected person.

Personally, if I thought someone could do more for himself/herself and I was the judge or on the jury, I would temporarily give the protected person one or two new responsibilities and see what kind of choices they make and how they handle their new freedoms, and have a court appointed guardian check in on them so they can report back to me in a month. In one month, I'd make the final decision if they can keep those freedoms or if the guardian needs to take over again! Then, if the protected person would want to, I'd let them try other responsibilities to see how they would manage those responsibilities for one month before I'd make a final choice, etc.

"Guardianship is not the best way to deal with emergencies." (Source: www.proguard.org)

Lawyer's fees are different depending on which lawyer you go to, but all lawyers do the same work in preventing or establishing a guardian in someone's life!

The person who pays the lawyer would be the proposed protected person, Superior Court, the county, or possibly the proposed guardian. There's a possibility that the cost can be shared among a couple of them.

There are legal duties of a guardian that are there to help identify a protected person's needs and to help them access the resources in the community.

A guardian getting a bond is one way to protect the client's money and property. A guardian of the estate can have control over a protected person's government money (and maybe the money they earn at work). If the guardian steals the protected person's money, the insurance company gives the money back. The guardian must pay the insurance company back and loses the privilege of being a guardian forever!

A second way to protect a person's estate is to put a "**block on a bank account**."

A "block on a bank account" means having two people watching over the protected person's money, etc. The judge can set boundaries around the guardian. For example, the judge can tell the guardian that he/she can't buy 'certain things' with the protected person's money even if they ask the guardian to buy it. The guardian sometimes still needs to get permission from the judge before buying some things.

A "block on an account" would have to be set up through a

bank or a credit union.

The third way of protecting the person's money is by reporting back to court. The judge will require receipts to prove where the money was spent for the person. The guardian has to make financial reports to the judge every 1-3 years to "the Court."

No matter what kind of guardian a protected person has, there are two kinds of legal papers to find out what the protected person is allowed to do and what the guardian must do:

- "Letters of Guardianship"
- "Order Appointing Guardian"

Even if a guardian is a full guardian, the guardian can't do whatever he/she pleases. The guardian has **no control** regarding if the protected person receives mental health services. The protected person or the court can choose or order him/her to get mental health services and/or counseling, but the guardian can't make that choice!

Guardians have no power over what style of clothes they wear *except* when their choice *endangers* their health! For example, a person can wear a dress, a skirt, leathers, chains, shirts with cigarette ads, Bible, beer, rock stars, or with moral/nice sayings on it! It is the **protected person's choice**!

There are some clothes that can give you attention you don't want such as being touched by people you don't know.

No matter how you are dressed, no one has the right to touch you without your permission. Some people will break the law and touch other people without their permission. By dressing modestly (covering your breasts and wearing clothes that go to the knee or below) people are less likely to bug you.

Ask your support team if you want to understand the health risks of dressing in certain ways.

However, it's illegal and wrong for a guardian to disapprove or approve of *certain* kinds of clothing based on the guardian's values and beliefs. If the guardian tries to tell them what they can and can't wear because of the guardian's values, the protected person has a responsibility to tell the GAL for two reasons (the guardian's personal values and personal fears).

The GAL will solve the problem for you in a way that is fair to everyone. It might be a compromise—both of you getting a little bit of what you want. The GAL might have to take your issues to their boss. The court is the supervisor over the GAL. The GAL is the guardian's supervisor.

Before the judge or jury makes their choice on the disagreement, they must research the issues. Anyone who has any knowledge or facts about the situation has an obligation to do or say something, but never based on personal opinions!

If anyone thinks a guardian and a protected person are not the right match for each other or that the establishment of a guardian is no longer needed, go to a GAL who will mediate or communicate between the guardian and the protected person to find out if the protected person can be responsible for anything new, or if the protected person needs a different guardian, or if they don't need a guardian at all.

RCW 11.88 explains the above information.

**The GAL will *try* to keep things out of the court and deal with it in the simplest way possible.

**If issues can be resolved outside of a courtroom, then keep it out to protect the individual's identity!

If anyone thinks there's a problem with the person who is seeking to become the guardian or who became the guardian, report it to the GAL. Report facts such as:

- Specific event(s)
- Dates things happened
- What you saw and heard
- How it affected the protected person

If you disagree with how a GAL handles your concern(s), tell the GAL's supervisor/boss. The (proposed) protected person has a right to a lawyer and you as an interested person should attend the hearing.

If you think an established guardian isn't meeting the needs/wants of a protected person, there are a couple of ways that I am aware of to deal with your concerns.

First, it is smart to get a lawyer to help you and them through the guardianship process for the modification or removal of a guardian.

Second, there is a possibility for seeing if the protected person *needs a less restrictive* kind of guardian and if a judge will allow the person to get *some new freedoms*; with the understanding of them having an advocate/teacher or someone else watching to see if they know how to stick to their own values! Basically, they go through the whole legal process with the court again. (It probably has to go through court to prevent taking advantage of someone financially or making sure their needs are met.)

An interested person can find the guardianship papers in the county courthouse. The papers should be in the office of the clerk. It is best to have the case number, even though the file can be found under the protected person's name.

It is possible for someone who is not a lawyer to stand up for a protected person. However, a lawyer is recommended because the legal papers are very hard to understand.

It helps a great deal to read the guardianship statutes RCW 11.88 and RCW 11.92. All the libraries in Washington State carry current versions of these State laws.

If you live in a different State, you can find the guardianship laws for your State in a law library. You can ask a work study student or practicum student at a college law library to help you or an advocacy organization like The Arc. The laws can be found online.

Guardianship and Intellectually Disabled Individuals

Not all people with disabilities need a guardian. If all the professionals agree that someone with a disability *needs* a guardian, then the person needs one. If all the professionals agree a person with a disability *doesn't need* a guardian, then the person does not need one, no matter what family and friends say. Either way it must go through the court!

A judge or jury must agree with the doctor's and/or family member's recommendation that someone needs a guardian. If the judge or jury disagrees, the person won't have a guardian!

*Work with all your professionals to get as much independence as you can and want!

Understanding Guardianship

Some States offer limited guardianships which allow a protected person to have control over part of their life and the limited guardian to have control over other parts of their life.

One of the roles of any kind of guardian is to include the protected person in making as many choices as they can.

Society believes in "safety and health." On the other hand, I like adventure, high risk, independence, and protecting health! I understand protecting everyone's health including mine!

My high-risk activity is flying in a small airplane—going extra high in the air and nose diving as a co-pilot. (I hate flying in commercial airplanes, but I do fly in them when it's necessary!)

Other high-risk activities could be skydiving, horseback riding, parachuting, etc. (These kinds of high-risk activities don't fall under the "safety and health rules.") If you can pay for it and someone tries to stop you, it's a valid complaint!

If I never did scary things like moving out of my parents' house, getting on a commercial airline, or going to college, I would never have become independent and I wouldn't be as mature as I am. Doing those things was a good compromise!

**Guardians must not "view" or "use" their position to limit a person's activity!

Where My Strength Lies

This chapter tells the **process** of how I came up with my **own belief system** and *how you might come up with your own belief system also*!

This chapter is written for the people who have not created their *own* belief system.

A belief system is when a choice becomes very hard to make, your basic beliefs are how you make choices! For example, if I had to make a choice between my disability beliefs, church beliefs, and my personal faith in God, the one that comes first is most important, then second, then third.

The following is being written to show the process of how I set my boundaries for everyday life choices. An example would be why I chose not to live with a man I am not married to. Another example is why I chose to tell the truth even if the truth hurts me.

It's also written to show the strength I have been given over time by exercising my beliefs. That is why I do not feel "ashamed" if I choose not to do to what a friend is pressuring me to do!

Health is another way to look at life. For example, what you eat—healthy or unhealthy, exercising, smoking, drinking, etc.

Faith is another way. However, faith in what or who? Is it a religion?

Some people just live by the "Golden Rule," "Treat others the way you want to be treated!"

I was raised with very high morals/standards. The "work ethics" were high for me. Work ethics means the standard you hold for doing things. You can have high work standards, in the middle or low standards. Standards can also be ethics.

The women in my mom's generation were stay-at-home moms if they could afford it! My parents gave money to organizations where they could, however, we always had enough money. In fact, if it was not for Child Protective Services discriminating against my mother's disability, my parents would have adopted a little girl my age so I would not have been an only child.

In 10th grade, my first boyfriend invited me to his youth group. I liked the way the people my age treated me at this church. The teenagers at this church had *more* of my parents' morals than the teenagers at my parents' church. (This does not mean my parents' church was bad or wrong. The church may have changed when they hired a youth pastor.)

Due to the youth group "peers" being nicer to each other at my church of choice than at the other church, I finally got the "**courage**" to ask my mom and dad if I could go to my boyfriend's youth group every Wednesday night.

The reason I asked instead of just going was to honor and respect my parents. My parents said I could go and I continued going to their church on Sundays.

As my parents realized I really did not like going to Sunday school, I asked them six months later if I could stop going to Sunday school, and they said okay. We still went to their church as a family. In another six months, I asked my parents if it was okay if I only attended my boyfriend's church on Sundays. I understood my parents were sad and happy to see me making my own choices in a safe way while *still living under their roof* where they could watch and protect me if needed.

Even when my choices are different, I am still a **valuable person** and **so are you**. However, it is smart to ask experienced people questions before you make a decision.

As a person under age 18 and not paying rent, I believe my parents had a right to know why I wanted to do certain things and who I was bringing into the house. This is practice for independence in a couple of ways. It's good to practice thinking through protecting your physical safety when making choices in life. It's also good to learn how to protect your property. This will help you to be able to protect other people's property also. Hopefully, you will be able to make **safe mistakes** and learn from your mistakes!

Who has authority over us?

- Religious leaders
- Politicians
- Bosses
- Guardians
- Police
- Caregivers
- Firefighters

What is the best way to respond to them and why?

Even though I was raised in a church and had switched churches, church was a social event I chose to do because it was a happy place to be.

My new church talked about having a personal relationship with Jesus Christ. At first, I did not understand this personal relationship stuff. If I went to church every Sunday and if I never smoked, or got drunk, or did illegal drugs, or went to casinos and gambled my money away, **and did my best to respect my parents**, what were these people talking about? In fact, the only man I gave permission to touch me is the man I married, *after* we got married.

With this being my childhood background, I made a choice to stand back and watch different people in this church and see how they dealt with hard times. I wanted to know what would happen to their faith in Jesus Christ if a family member got really sick or if they found out they were going to have to move out of town.

It was very interesting *watching* these people to see if what they *said* matched their walk with God when life was not going 'their way.' In fact, it seemed to me that I was doing all the things that a 'Christian' is supposed to do, like tell the truth. "Honesty is the best policy." With high morals and high standards like mine, I still did not understand the *need* for what the people at this church called a 'personal relationship with Jesus Christ.'

I, by my choice, started talking to different people and asking questions about why having a personal relationship with Jesus Christ is so important to them individually.

My questions were: What makes God so real in your life? What were you like before you accepted Jesus Christ into your life? What are you like today, now that you have a personal relationship with God? How long have you had this personal relationship? (My reason for asking the last question was because a person who has only been a Christian for one month will act different than the Christian who has known God for five years, ten years or more.) Also, I asked people who were old enough to be my grandparents, my parents, and those who were my age.

This was my process! I suggest this for when you are making an informed choice to help you decide if you want to make the same choice as others.

Finally, I went to a three-day youth retreat and **understood for myself** this message of Jesus Christ that my church friends had been trying to explain to me.

It took the process of watching church people to see if they were 'for real' and asking questions of different people before my heart and ears were willing to listen regarding their personal relationship with Jesus Christ.

The difference is Jesus is in my heart and ruling my heart instead of just knowing in my head that HE is alive and following His commandments by "duty."

Duty means something you have to do like go to work. Now my heart **wants** to follow His commandments and live a godly life.

Now that I went through the process of choosing what *my* belief system is and will continue to be since March 1988 until today (2022) and probably will be for the rest of my life, I need to learn to see life through God's eyes. I had to learn not to be afraid if I made a mistake, like saying a bad word. I had to learn to read the Bible and pray **every day**.

Having your **own** belief system should be *consistent* with what you believe when other people *challenge you* to do things you think are wrong.

Now that I chose to have this personal relationship with God, I stopped feeling bad for making different choices and I did not feel ashamed for making mistakes because I could forgive myself and others. When I make mistakes, I can also learn from them!

How do you make *all* your decisions related to smoking, drinking alcohol, taking illegal drugs or *not* doing these things, etc.? If you say health is how you decide if something is good or bad, remember, different doctors say different things. Also, different medical reports come out with different findings or new findings.

If you say it depends on what the law says, remember that our laws could change at any level such as city, county, State or federal levels. For example, about 15 years ago, I believe smoking was 100% legal. For the people who have been smoking for 15 years, these people will be fighting an addiction to stop smoking **if smoking** or other things become illegal *that were legal in the past*!

If you make your choices by your religion, then think about who chose your religion. Was it you who chose, your family, your friends, or your guardian? Does your church, synagogue, mass, etc. encourage you to read the "Holy Book," such as a Bible or do they not encourage you to read the "Holy Book" and to only listen and trust what the pastor, rabbi, priest, and leaders in the faith are saying?

Just like any other human beings in authority in our lives such as our parents, family, caregivers, guardians, etc., *everyone makes mistakes*! This is why it is important for me to have a personal relationship with God and be under the authority of a church leadership of *my* choice.

Do you know God personally? He has a plan so we can know Him. He is waiting for you to answer "His call."

"Call" means that God is willing to listen if you pray to Him.

You can get forgiveness from everything you have done wrong in the past. You can also know for sure that you have "everlasting life" through faith/trust in God's only Son, Jesus Christ.

What stops us from knowing God personally? Lack of education of who God is and not knowing what He has done for us!

If you want to understand how to meet and know God personally, *read on*!

(Get a Bible to make sure what is being written here is also what the Bible says.)

Here are some **truths** that will help you find out how to meet and know God personally and join in the everlasting life that He promised.

#1 God loves you and created you to know Him personally!

GOD'S LOVE

"For God so loved the world, that He gave His one and only Son that whoever believes in Him should not perish, but have eternal life" (John 3:16). "Perish" means spiritual death.

(If you have a Bible that uses the term "eternal life," know that the phrase "everlasting life" means the same thing as "eternal life." Other Bibles use "everlasting life." For me, everlasting life is easier to understand and explain.)

GOD'S PLAN

"Now this is eternal life: that they may know you, the only true God, and Jesus Christ, whom you have sent" (John 17:3 NIV).

"NIV" means New International Version of the Bible.

What stops us from knowing God personally?

People are 'sinful' and separated from God, so we cannot know Him personally or experience His love.

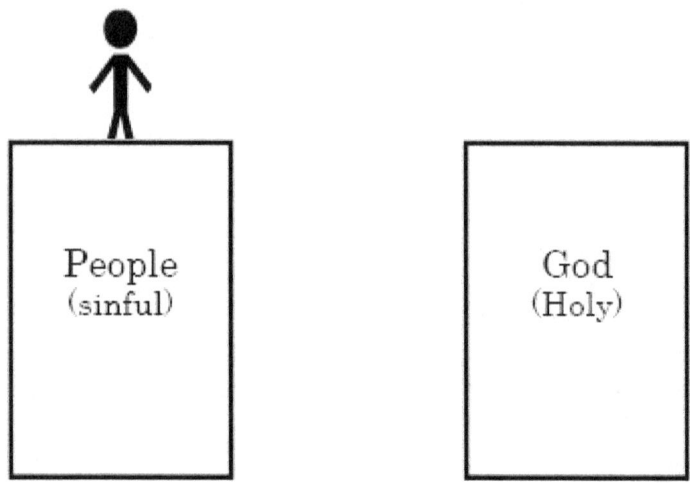

"Sin" is breaking God's laws or "sin" is going against God's laws. Either one of these could happen accidently or on purpose. Even if it is an accident, it's sin!

#2A The next truth is people are sinful.
"For all have sinned and fall short of the glory of God" (Romans 3:23).

"Fall short" or "falling short" means not meeting God's standard of perfection, set by God.

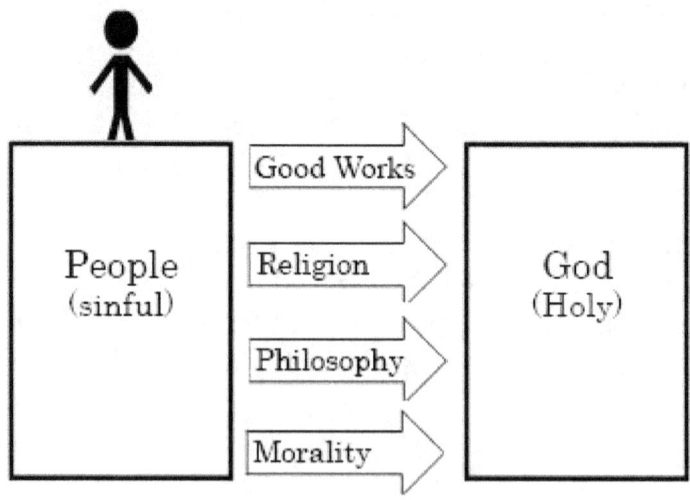

The picture above shows different ways that sinful people *try* to reach God.

(Going to church at least once a week, living a life with very good behavior and helping others are good, **but not with the purpose of reaching God!**)

People were made to have a relationship with God; but because of their own "self-will," they chose to go their own way and break their relationship with God.

"Self-will" means choosing to go your own way and do your own thing. "Self-will" can also be seen when what you are doing and saying is for your own self-pleasure or if you show a "passive indifference" towards God.

"Passive indifference" means anything goes; you have no opinion (in this case, not caring about the things of God, faith, and sin).

Both doing and saying things that do not make God happy and not caring about the things of God are "evidence of sin."

"Evidence" means facts.

#2B People are separated.

"Separated" means apart or divided.

"For the wages of sin is death" (Romans 6:23). The Bible is talking about spiritual separation/death from God.

The next truth says the *only way* to reach God is through Jesus Christ.

#3 Jesus Christ is God's only way to bridge the gap between God's perfection and people's sinfulness and wrongdoing!

Through Him alone we can know God ***personally*** and experience His love. He died ***in our place***.

"But God demonstrates His own love toward us, in that while we were yet sinners, Christ died for us" (Romans 5:8).

He rose from the dead.

"Christ died for our sins...He was buried...He was raised on the third day, according to the Scriptures...He appeared to

209

Peter, then to the twelve. After that He appeared to more than 500..." (1 Corinthians 15:3-66).

He is the only way to God.

"Jesus said to him, 'I am the way, and the truth, and the life; no one comes to the Father, but through Me'" (John14:6).

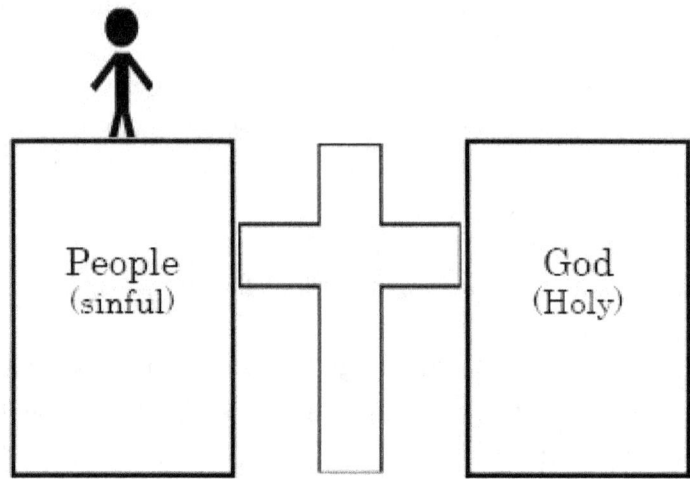

This picture shows how God reached down to sinful people by sending His Son, Jesus Christ to die on the cross in our place to pay the "penalty" for our sins.

"Penalty" means legal punishment for a crime, in this case, breaking God's laws.

It is not just enough to know these true facts in your head. Each person must make "their **own choice**" to receive Jesus Christ as "Savior" and "Lord," then they can know God personally and experience His love.

"Savior" means one who saves. (Savior with a capitol "S" means God.)

"Lord" means God having 100% control over people's lives who accept Him as Lord.

The next truth is **you must choose** for yourself to accept or reject Jesus Christ.

"But as many as received Him, to them He gave the right to become children of God, even to those who believe in His name" (John 1:12).

"For by grace you have been saved through faith; and that not of yourselves, it is a gift of God; not as a result of works, that no one should boast" (Ephesians 2:8-9).

God hates proud words!

When we receive Christ, we experience a "new birth." (You can read John 3:1-8.)

"New birth" means spiritual birth.

We receive Christ by personal invitation.

Christ said, *"Behold, I stand at the door and knock; if anyone hears My voice and opens the door, I will come in to him"* (Revelation 3:20).

Receiving Christ involves turning to God and away from yourself (which is repenting from sin) and trusting Christ to come into our lives to forgive our sins, and make us the kind of people He wants us to be.

It is not enough to only know and accept these facts in your head: that Jesus Christ is the Son of God, and that He died on the cross for our sins (with no heart experience).

It is not enough to only have an emotional experience or good feelings or a heart experience (with no facts).

We receive Christ by faith (into our heart) as an act of the will.

"... if you confess with your mouth that, Jesus is Lord, and believe in your heart that God raised Him from the dead, you will be saved" (Romans (10:9).

The following two circles represent a "self-centered life" or a "Christ-centered life." Here is what the symbols represent:

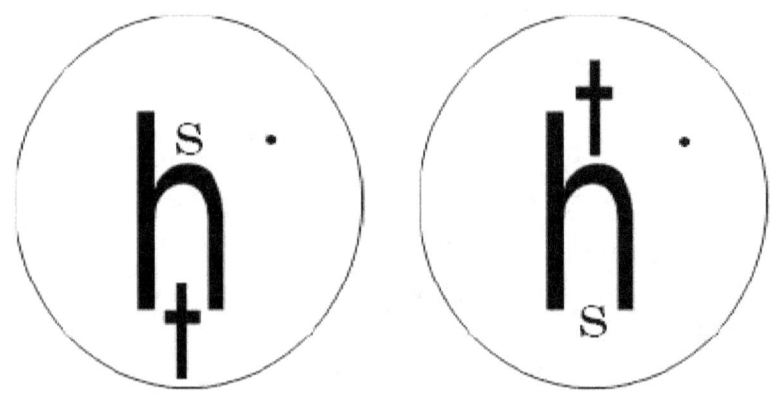

h = throne, s = self, † = Christ, and • = interests directed by who is on the throne.

      Self-directed life   Christ-directed life

Which circle best represents your life?

Which circle would you like to have represent your life?

The following explains how you can invite Jesus Christ into your life.

You can receive Christ now by faith through prayer!

(Prayer is talking with God.)

God knows your heart and is not as concerned with your words as He is with the attitude of your heart. The following is a suggested prayer:

"Lord Jesus, I want to know You personally. Thank You for dying on the cross for my sins. I open the door of my life and receive You. Thank You for forgiving my sins and giving me everlasting life. Take control of the throne of my life. Make me the kind of person You want me to be!"

Does this prayer express the desire of your heart or not?

If it does, pray this prayer right now and Christ will come into your heart, as He promised.

How to know that Jesus Christ is in your life?

Did you receive Christ into your life? According to His promise in Revelation 3:20, where is Christ right now? Is He inside or outside of you? Christ said that He would come into your life and be your friend, so you can know Him personally.

Would He mislead you? On what authority do you know that God has answered your prayer? (The trustworthiness or honesty of God Himself and His Word.)

The Bible promises everlasting/eternal life to all who receive Christ.

"And the witness is this that God has given us eternal life and this life is in the Son. He who does have the Son of God has the life; he who does not have the Son of God does not have the life. These things I have written to you who believe in the name of the Son of God, in order that you may know that you have eternal life" (1 John 5:11 - 13).

Thank God often that Christ is in your life, and that He will never leave you (Hebrew 13:5). You can know, on the basis of the promise that Christ lives in you and that you have eternal life, from the very moment you invite Him in. He will not deceive you.

An important reminder…

Do not depend on feelings.

The promise of God's Word, the Bible—not our feelings is our authority. The Christian life is lived by faith (trust) in God Himself and His Word.

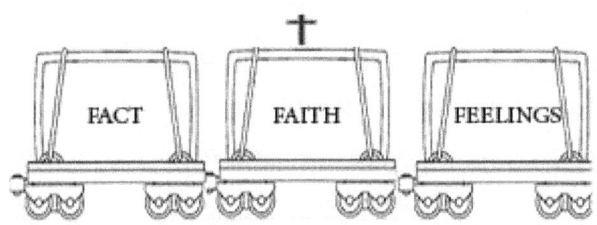

This picture of a train shows the relationship between fact (God and His Word), faith (our trust in God and His Word), and feelings (the result of our faith and obedience). (John 14:21)

The train will run with or without the caboose. However, it is useless to try to pull the caboose. In the same way, we as

Christians do not depend on feelings or emotions, but we place our faith (trust) in the honesty of God and the promises of His Word.

Now that you have entered into a personal relationship with Christ:

The moment that you received Christ by faith, as an act of the will many things happened, including the following:

1) Christ came into your life (Revelation 3:20 and Colossians 1:27).
2) Your sins were forgiven (Colossians 1:14).
3) You became a child of God (John 1:12).
4) You received everlasting life (John 5:24).
5) You began the great adventure for which God created you (John 10:10, 2 Corinthians 5:17 and 1 Thessalonians 5:18).

Can you think of anything more wonderful that could happen to you than entering into a personal relationship with Jesus Christ? Would you like to thank God in prayer right now for what He has done for you? By thanking God, you demonstrate your faith.

To enjoy your new relationship with God, spiritual growth results from trusting Jesus Christ. *"The righteous shall live by faith"* (Galatians 3:11).

A life of faith will enable you to trust God increasing with every detail of your life, and to practice the following growth:

G   Go to God in prayer daily (John 15:7).
R   Read God's Word daily (Acts 17:11) beginning with the Gospel of John.
O   Obey God moment by moment (John 14:21).
W   Witness for Christ by your life and words (Matthew 4:19 and John 15:8).
T   Trust God for every detail of your life (Proverbs 3:5).
H   Holy Spirit – Allow Him to control and empower your

daily life and witness (Galatians 5:16-17 and Acts 1:8).

Fellowship in a good church.

God's Word encourages us to get together with others who believe in Jesus Christ as their Savior and Lord. (Read Hebrews 10:25 with someone else.) Several logs burn brightly together, but put one aside on the cold hearth, and the fire goes out.

So it is with our relationship with other Christians. If you do not belong to a good church, do not wait to be invited. Take the initiative; call the pastor of a nearby church where Christ is honored and His Word is preached. Start this week and make plans to attend.

Thank you for taking the time to read this book. If you have accepted Jesus Christ into your heart, please send me an email at responsiblyindependent@yahoo.com.

About the Author

Having been born with lots of disabilities, Tiffani Harvey struggled with people in authority who thought she was not able to do very much. She has done a lot!

Because of her faith in God and training in self advocacy, she has depended on God and gained knowledge of government and business to advocate and to protect herself. She wants to pass these lessons on.

Tiffani is married with two children. She spent 18 years writing her story before she found a group of writers to help her.

If you found this book to be helpful, please tell others about it and email the author to let her know at responsiblyindependent@yahoo.com.